SALAD
THE TASTE OF SUMMER

Photography Ashley Barber
Styling Michelle Gorry

A BAY BOOKS PUBLICATION
An imprint of HarperCollinsPublishers

First published in Australia in 1988 by Bay Books
Reprinted in 1992, 1993

Bay Books, of
CollinsAngus&Robertson Publishers Pty Limited
A division of HarperCollinsPublishers (Australia) Pty Limited
25 Ryde Road, Pymble NSW 2073, Australia
HarperCollinsPublishers (New Zealand) Limited
31 View Road, Glenfield, Auckland 10, New Zealand
HarperCollinsPublishers Limited
77– 85 Fulham Palace Road, London W6 8JB, United Kingdom

ISBN 1 86378 020 3

Typeset by Savage Typeset, Brisbane
Printed in Australia by Griffin Press, Adelaide

8 7 6 5 4 3
97 96 95 94 93

SALAD
THE TASTE OF SUMMER

Compiled by Janice Baker

Bay Books
An imprint of HarperCollinsPublishers

Contents

WHAT GOES INTO A SALAD?

*Tired of plain old salads? With this book, salads need never be boring again.
We give you a comprehensive guide to salad ingredients, including a run
down on those unusual vegetables you've always wondered about
and didn't know how to use.
Our herb list explains how these health-giving plants add piquancy to any
salad and the section on different types of oils and vinegars gives you
a good idea of the variety of dressings you can make.
How do you make the perfect vinaigrette? It's all here, along with recipes for
Italian dressing, exotic mayonnaises and horseradish cream.*

Salad greens

Chicory: (Belgian endive or whitloof) Tightly clustered, smooth white leaves with yellow tips. Slightly bitter flavour.

Curly endive: Sold in large bunches. The long leaves graduate from pale, greeny yellow to dark green. Use only the paler heart and stalks. Bitter flavour.

Escarole: Long frilly leaves. Use only the centre young leaves. Slightly bitter.

Butter lettuce: Soft, smallish lettuce. Mild flavour. Also called round lettuce.

Cos or Romaine lettuce: Elongated head of dark green oval leaves and a crisp pale green heart. Has a pungent flavour and stays crisp.

Iceberg or crisp head lettuce: A large lettuce with crisp outer leaves and a firm sweet heart. This is the basis of many a salad as the leaves will stay crisp,

Mignonette lettuce: Soft, smallish leaves with edges tinged pink to red.

Mustard and cress: Seeds are usually sown together and eaten at the seedling stage. Sold in punnets. Snip off the tops as required.

Radicchio: This slightly bitter red-green chicory is much loved throughout Italy. Sold as tiny, single loose leaves either wholly green or tinged with red. Some varieties come as a slightly conical head.

Rocket: Small, acidic, dark green leaves. Sold while the plant is still very young.

Silverbeet: Often called spinach, beet or chard. Used in salads only when leaves are very young. Discard the white stalk. The older, larger leaves should be steamed and eaten hot.

Spinach: (English) Dark green leaves. Eaten raw in salads when leaves are young and fresh. Stalk may be eaten as well.

Watercress: Has a pungent, slightly peppery taste. Pick over the bunch using only young leaves and tender stems for salads. Whatever remains will make an excellent soup.

Radicchio

Chicory

Butter lettuce

Silverbeet

Mignonette lettuce

Watercress

Spinach

Curly endive

Mustard cress

Rocket

Cos lettuce

Other salad vegetables

Alfalfa sprouts: Sold in punnets or loose and eaten at the seedling stage when full of vitamins and minerals. Keep refrigerated once purchased as they continue to grow. Simply pull required amount from punnet.

Artichoke hearts: Sold in oil. Delightful sliced into a salad.

Artichokes: (globe or common) Artichokes make a good container for an individual salad. Pull off any coarse outer leaves. Cut off top third of the artichoke. Remove hairy choke and cook in boiling, salted water (made slightly acidic with a dash of vinegar or squeeze of lemon juice) for 20–40 minutes, depending on their size. Cool and serve filled with a vinaigrette dressing or fill with a salad of your choice.

Asparagus: A popular addition to salads. Blanch in boiling, salted water and refresh before using; or simply steam lightly. May be used whole if young, or cut into spears.

Avocado: This pear-shaped fruit has a delicate yet very distinctive flavour. Best stored in a cool place (rather than in a refrigerator). Eat at room temperature for full flavour. Slice just before using — otherwise rub the cut surfaces with lemon juice or vinaigrette.

Baby squash: Eaten when very young and tender. Green or yellow in colour. Similar in flavour to a baby zucchini.

Beans: Crisp, young green runner beans need only topping, tailing and rinsing before use. May be sliced or left whole.

Bean sprouts: These are sprouted mung beans used when the sprout is about 3 cm long. Should be crisp and sweet-smelling when purchased. Pinch off the dry, stringy end of the root before using.

Cabbage
Chinese cabbage: Elongated cabbage with green-edged leaves. Heart nearly white. Crinkly leaves may be shredded and used raw.
Red cabbage: Usually cooked with vinegar. May be finely shredded for coleslaw, adding a beautiful, purple-red colour to the slaw.
Round head cabbage: Smooth pale green leaves.
Savoy cabbage: Has dark green wrinkled leaves with a firmly packed head. Good shredded in coleslaw.
White cabbage: Usually used for coleslaw or sauerkraut.

Capsicum: (Bell peppers) May be green, red, yellow or black. Use raw. Halve, remove seeds and woody stem. Slice or chop. The sweet peppery flavour is very distinctive.

Carrots: Use young, crisp carrots for salads. Peel if necessary. Grate, julienne or leave whole if very small.

Cauliflower: For salads, break into florets and blanch in boiling salted water. Drain and refresh under cold, running water and dry well.

Celery: Sold in whole or half heads. May be sliced or cut into sticks. For celery curls, split 6 cm lengths halfway down each piece a few times. Repeat at other end and plunge into iced water. Leave until curled and crisp. Always keep celery refrigerated especially in summer.

Cucumber
Apple cucumber: Small, creamy white and oval-shaped. Peel before using.
Green or ridge cucumber: Peel, leaving a little of the green skin (this is said to help with digestion). The surface may be scored with a fork. May be sliced into rounds or halved and seeded then sliced. Some people still like to lightly salt the slices to remove indigestible juices. Allow to stand for 30 minutes, drain and rinse well with cold water.
Lebanese cucumber: Small, smooth-skinned green cucumber.
Telegraph cucumber: A long, thin, dark green variety of cucumber, crisp with a good flavour.

Garlic: Choose firm, young white or purple bulbs when purchasing. Remove papery skin by crushing clove with back of a knife. Continue crushing and add a pinch salt. The salt acts as an abrasive to pulp the flesh while also absorbing pungent juices. Use a garlic press to crush if you prefer.

Kohlrabi: A cabbage-turnip type of vegetable either purple or green in colour. The thickened stem is eaten and has a delicate turnip flavour. May be boiled or eaten raw. Add to salads grated or sliced. Delicious offset by horseradish.

Mushrooms: Use firm, white button mushrooms or caps in a salad. Brush off any compost (don't rinse) and trim stalk end. Serve whole or sliced.

Onions
Shallot: (scallion, sometimes called green onions) Trim away roots and peel dry outer leaves before using. Fresh onion flavour.
Spring onion: These have a white bulb with long green tops. Use white bulb with a little of the green stem finely chopped. Sold in bunches. Mild onion flavour.
Spanish onion: Mild, sweet juicy onion with a red colour which makes an attractive addition to salads.
True French shallot: Small brownish bulb with a mild onion flavour. Used mainly in sautees.
White onions: Round, firm and white-fleshed with a dry white papery skin. Peel before use. Strong, hot, pungent flavour. Use sparingly.

Radish: Firm, crisp, red bulbs, sold in bunches. Tops should be fresh-looking. Slice or serve whole with a few small, green sprigs still attached. Remove stringy root.

Snake beans: Sold in bunches. Slice and blanch before using in a salad.

Tomatoes: Always use tomatoes at room temperature. Look for a good red colour and firm flesh when using in salads. Whole cherry tomatoes or tom thumbs are a welcome addition to any salad. Also available are the small, yellow pear-shaped tomatoes, which have a surprisingly good flavour.

Round head cabbage

Yellow pear-shaped
tomatoes

Chinese cabbage

Red cabbage

Whole cherry tomatoes

Alfalfa sprouts

Shallots

Savoy cabbage

Asparagus

Telegraph cucumber

Apple cucumber

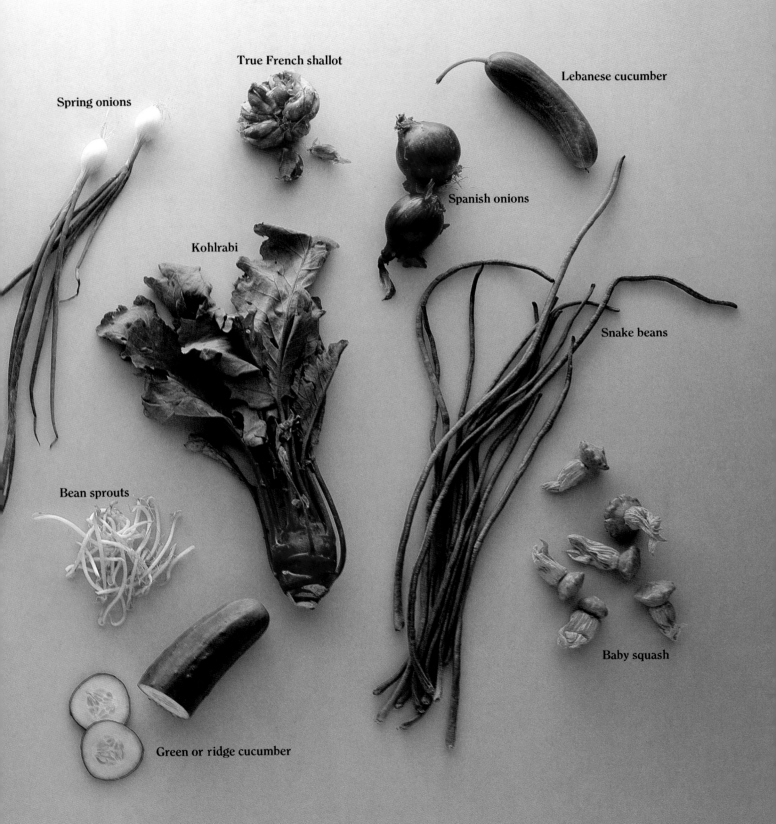

True French shallot

Spring onions

Lebanese cucumber

Spanish onions

Kohlrabi

Snake beans

Bean sprouts

Baby squash

Green or ridge cucumber

Herbs

Herbs play an important part in any salad. They are used to add flavour, texture and decoration. The appearance and nature of a salad can be changed simply by varying the kinds of herbs added, or by the flavour of oil or vinegar used. Fresh herbs are readily available at the greengrocer's or you might have a small herb garden. Always try to use fresh rather than dried herbs in salads as the flavour is milder.

Basil

Basil (or sweet basil): Has large aromatic leaves and is sold in bunches or as seedlings in punnets. Its strong distinctive flavour combines well with tomatoes. Always snip or cut so as not to bruise the leaves.

Bush basil: A small-leaved plant with a mild flavour. Usually sold in punnets as seedlings.

Purple basil: Similar to sweet basil, used for its attractive colour.

Borage: Adds a fresh, cucumber-like taste when used in salads. Snip the leaves over a salad and use the pretty, mauve flowers to decorate.

Chervil: An annual from Russia and the Middle East. Use fresh or dried leaves.

Chives: Slender, green, hollow chives are readily available. The whole stem is used. Snip into a salad or use whole as a garnish. Mild onion flavour. Their flowers also make an attractive garnish.

Coriander: The fresh, frilly leaves of coriander are sometimes called 'Chinese parsley'. Coriander has a very distinctive aroma and flavour. Teams well with Asian-style salads and fruits, such as pears and mangoes. The seeds are often used to flavour oils and vinegars.

Dill: A member of the parsley family. The seeds and the leaves can be used, fresh or dried. Also found in dill pickles and dill vinegar.

Marjoram: (wild oregano) Not as strong as oregano in flavour and slightly sweeter. When fresh it teams well with tomatoes and olives. May be used to flavour oils and vinegars.

Mint: Round or common mint is found growing wild in many gardens. Spearmint — named because of its long, narrow leaves — is usually sold commercially. There are over 40 varieties of mint. This fresh-tasting herb is so flavoursome that it is not usually used with any other herb apart from parsley (as in Tabouli).

Oregano: Usually used in Italian cooking. Not normally added to a salad, but may be used to flavour an olive oil or vinegar.

Parsley: (Curly leaf or flat-leaved Italian parsley) An essential herb for any salad. Use freshly chopped for a good source of Vitamin C. Look for a good, green colour. Sold in a bunch. Fresh parsley should be sweet smelling.

Rosemary: Long, thin, deep green leaves with a spicy, mint flavour and aroma. Use leaves fresh or dried (fresh leaves are best in salads). Buy in sprigs.

Sage: Grows in woody bushes of grey-green leaves with tiny blue flowers. Use leaves fresh or dried.

Tarragon: Long, thin leaves along a stem. Sold in bunches. French variety has a good, delicate flavour. Delicious when used to flavour oils or vinegars. Combines well with chicken, eggs, pears and potatoes.

Thyme

Common thyme: Often used to flavour oils or vinegars. Sometimes used fresh over salads.

Lemon thyme: Has a strong lemon flavour, delicious in a chicken salad. Also used to flavour oils and vinegars.

Curly leaf parsley

Flat-leaved Italian parsley

Bush basil

Dill

Mint

Basil

Sage

Coriander

Lemon thyme

Thyme

Rosemary

Variegated thyme

Marjoram

Chives

Oregano

Garlic chives

Tarragon

Vinegar

Vinegar is the liquid product of an acid fermentation process of various grains and fruits. For instance, white wine vinegar is the acidic product of white wine, likewise cider vinegar of apple juice and malt vinegar of malt liquor.

Vinegars vary greatly in strength and flavour, according to their base. Vinegar is an essential ingredient in salads. The fresh acid cleans the palate and brings out the full flavour of salad vegetables.

Lemon juice, yoghurt, buttermilk and soy sauce also provide this element when used in a salad, however vinegar is the main ingredient used.

The most popular vinegars for use in salad dressings are: champagne vinegar, cider vinegar, red wine vinegar, rice vinegar and white wine vinegar.

Fruit vinegar: Combine 4 cups wine vinegar with 2 cups soft fruits such as raspberries, strawberries, blueberries, pears, peaches or plums. Stir to lightly bruise the fruit. Cover and leave to infuse for 2 days. Bring to just boiling point. Strain the vinegar through a double piece of cheesecloth into clean sterilised bottles. Cork and label.

Herb infused vinegar: Combine 4 cups of wine vinegar with ½ cup bruised fresh herbs in a glass or earthenware bowl. Cover and leave to infuse for 2 weeks. Strain through a double piece of cheesecloth into clean sterilised bottles. Add a sprig of the fresh herb to each bottle. Cork and label.

Left to right: red wine vinegar, herb infused vinegar, corn oil, virgin olive oil, walnut oil, sesame oil, grapeseed oil

Oil

The foundation of a good dressing is the oil and vinegar. The carefully balanced combination of these is important to bring out the full flavour of the salad. The kind of oil used depends greatly on the type of salad.

Almond oil, hazelnut oil and walnut oil: These are a delight to use in a dressing. They have a good nutty flavour that complements many a salad.

Chilli oil: Warm 2 cups olive oil and pour into a clean bottle with 1–2 tablespoons chopped Birds-eye chillies. Cap and store in a cool, dark place. Ready to use after 2 weeks.

Corn oil, peanut oil, safflower oil and sunflower oil: All polyunsaturated oils. They are light with little flavour and may be used in combination with one of the other more full-bodied oils to lighten a particular dressing. Used alone they tend to lack flavour.

Grapeseed oil: Has a good nutty flavour and is light.

Herb infused oil: Warm 2 cups olive oil and pour into a clean jar with ¼ cup fresh herbs. Cover and leave to seep for 2 weeks. Strain the oil through a fine cheesecloth into a bottle and store in a cool, dark place until required.

Olive oil: Possibly the most widely used oil, not only in salads but also in cooking. Its range of flavours and smoothness makes it the supreme oil. The oil is produced from pressing ripe to not-so-ripe olives. Grades vary with each pressing. Extra virgin oil is the best as it is the first oil released from the pressing. It is clear, often green, with a good, strong olive flavour. Use olive oil when you want that distinctive olive flavour. It's worth experimenting with olive oils to find one that suits your tastes and requirements.

Sesame oil: Has a strong sesame flavour. Use sparingly as it can sometimes overpower the salad.

Dressings

A vinaigrette may be made in a number of ways. Below, we give you the basic dressing. From this recipe — by varying the mustard, vinegar or oil — you will achieve a different dressing every time.

Vary the basic recipe by using a pinch dried mustard in place of the Dijon-style mustard: use a grainy seed mustard, a German-style mustard or a herb mustard. There are a number of herb vinegars on the market, so use these in place of white wine vinegar.

Fruit vinegars such as raspberry or strawberry vinegar, are popular or use lemon juice as a vinegar substitute. Always taste the dressing before you add all the vinegar, because some are more acidic than others.

Using a different oil changes a dressing dramatically. The classic dressing is always made with a good olive oil, but you might like to use a lighter seed oil or one of the many nut oils available, such as walnut or hazelnut. These have a rich nutty flavour and complement salad greens very well.

And, of course, garlic in any shape or form is a must for a hearty dressing, either used to flavour the oil, or added raw to the dressing. Chopped fresh herbs look and taste good — but use the dressing within a couple of hours of adding these, otherwise add the herbs to the oil for extra flavour.

Left to right: Italian Dressing, Walnut Dressing, Vinaigrette

ITALIAN DRESSING

*2 tablespoons Italian or French
wine vinegar
½ clove garlic, crushed
salt and freshly ground pepper to
taste
1 cup olive oil
1 tablespoon finely chopped
parsley*

Combine the vinegar, garlic, salt and ground pepper. Gradually whisk in the oil and garnish with the parsley.

Makes 1½ cups

WALNUT DRESSING 1

*2 teaspoons Dijon-style mustard
salt and freshly ground pepper to
taste
2 tablespoons white wine vinegar
½ cup walnut oil
½ cup safflower oil*

Combine mustard, salt, ground pepper and vinegar in a bowl then gradually whisk in the oils.

Makes 1½ cups

WALNUT DRESSING 2

*1 tablespoon red wine vinegar
½ cup walnut oil
1 clove garlic, crushed with a
little salt
freshly ground pepper to taste*

Combine all ingredients and shake well in a jar.

Makes 1½ cups

MAYONNAISE

*3 egg yolks
1 tablespoon Dijon-style mustard
pinch salt
freshly ground pepper
2 tablespoons lemon juice
1½–2 cups good olive oil*

Place the egg yolks, mustard, salt, pepper and lemon juice in a container and blend or whisk mixture for 1 minute. Add the oil in a slow, steady stream while continuing to blend. When all the oil is incorporated scrape down the sides. Taste for seasoning and spoon into a bowl. Cover with plastic wrap and set aside until ready to use. Mayonnaise will keep for a few days in a cool place or for a week refrigerated.

Makes 2 cups
Note: Throughout the book wherever 'mayonnaise' is referred to, see this recipe or use bought mayonnaise.

VINAIGRETTE

To make ⅓ cup
1 tablespoon Dijon-style mustard
1 tablespoon white wine vinegar
salt and freshly ground black
pepper
3–4 tablespoons olive oil

To make 1 cup
1–2 tablespoons Dijon-style
mustard
3 tablespoons white wine vinegar
salt and freshly ground pepper
¾ cup olive oil

Place mustard in a bowl and whisk in the white wine vinegar. Season with salt and freshly ground pepper and gradually whisk in olive oil, until mixture thickens. Adjust seasoning to taste.

AIOLI (GARLIC MAYONNAISE)

12–16 cloves garlic, peeled
3 egg yolks
salt and freshly ground black
pepper
2 cups olive oil
juice 2 lemons

Puree garlic. Add egg yolks, salt and pepper. Blend until smooth. Continue to blend, adding oil in a thin, steady stream. As the sauce thickens, add the lemon juice and adjust seasoning. A little lukewarm water may be added if necessary to achieve the right consistency.

Makes 2 cups

HORSERADISH SOUR CREAM DRESSING

300 mL sour cream
3 tablespoons grated horseradish
salt and freshly ground black
pepper

Beat sour cream with horseradish. Season with salt and freshly ground pepper.

Makes 1½ cups

CURRIED MAYONNAISE

1 shallot
2 tablespoons olive oil
1 tablespoon good curry powder
2 teaspoons tomato paste
½ cup water
2 teaspoons mango chutney
1 cup mayonnaise (see recipe)

Chop shallot and soften in olive oil. Add the curry powder and cook for a minute. Add the tomato paste and water and simmer for 3–4 minutes, reducing the volume to 2 tablespoons. Stir in the mango chutney and cool. When cold fold through the mayonnaise.

Left to right: Curried Mayonnaise, Roquefort Dressing, Thousand Island Dressing, Tzatziki Dressing, Pesto Mayonnaise

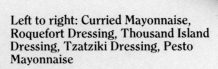

THOUSAND ISLAND DRESSING

1 cup mayonnaise (see recipe)
¼ cup chopped green olives
3 tablespoons chopped capers
1 small onion, finely grated
1 tablespoon tomato paste
½ teaspoon chilli sauce

Combine all ingredients together.

Makes 1½ cups

ROQUEFORT DRESSING

100 g Roquefort cheese
¼ cup cream
1 cup mayonnaise (see recipe)

Crumble Roquefort cheese into a small bowl. Beat in cream until smooth and gradually add the mayonnaise.

Makes 1¼ cups

TZATZIKI DRESSING

1 medium-sized green cucumber
2 cloves garlic, crushed with salt
1½ cups unflavoured yoghurt
freshly ground black pepper
1 tablespoon chopped fresh mint

Peel cucumber, halve and scoop out seeds. Grate cucumber finely into a bowl. Drain away some of the cucumber liquor. Add the garlic and yoghurt. Beat with a wooden spoon until liquid. Season with black pepper and stir through chopped mint.

Makes 2 cups

PESTO MAYONNAISE

3 egg yolks
1 teaspoon Dijon-style mustard
1 tablespoon white wine vinegar
3 cloves garlic, peeled
1½ cups olive oil
salt and freshly ground pepper
¾ cup fresh basil leaves
¼ cup parsley leaves
¼ cup grated Parmesan cheese

Place egg yolks in a container and blend with mustard, vinegar and garlic. Blend until smooth. Still blending, add the oil in a slow steady stream, until a thick mayonnaise has formed. Season well with salt and freshly ground pepper. Add the basil and parsley leaves, blend until smooth. Add the Parmesan cheese and blend until combined. The sauce should be of coating consistency, if it is too thick, add a little water.

Makes 2 cups

SIMPLY STARTERS

*Delight your guests with entree dishes that display style and imagination.
It can be as simple as Smoked Turkey and Pawpaw with Cranberry Mayonnaise.
We've also included favourites like Artichoke Hearts Stuffed with
Camembert, and Eggplant Shells with Savoury Tomato Filling.
All these dishes are quick and easy to prepare, yet the finished product
looks like a culinary masterpiece.*

ARTICHOKE HEARTS STUFFED WITH CAMEMBERT

*8 canned artichoke hearts,
chokes removed
150 g Camembert, diced
120 g asparagus, trimmed,
peeled and cut into 2.5 cm pieces
1 cup cream
¼ cup chopped shallots
60 g butter
1 large tomato, peeled, seeded
and chopped
2 teaspoons chopped fresh dill*

Arrange artichoke hearts in ovenproof dish. Fill hearts with diced Camembert. Cover with foil and warm in oven. Quickly cook asparagus in boiling, salted water until tender, then drain and rinse under cold water. Puree with 2 tablespoons cream. Saute shallots in butter then add asparagus puree, tomato, dill and remaining cream. Reduce the sauce, gradually, until thickened then season to taste and spoon over the artichoke hearts and serve.

Serves 4

CHERRY TOMATOES FILLED WITH HUMMUS

*1 cup chick peas, soaked
overnight
½ cup tahini
1 clove garlic, crushed
3 tablespoons lemon juice
salt, cayenne pepper and paprika
1 punnet cherry tomatoes
2 tablespoons chopped fresh
parsley
1½ tablespoons olive oil*

Cook chick peas in 1½ cups water to cover. Bring to the boil, reduce heat and simmer for 1½ hours until tender. Drain and reserve liquid. Reserve ½ cup chick peas for garnish.

Puree remaining peas with garlic. Blend in tahini and lemon juice, then add a little of the reserved cooking liquid to make a thick, creamy consistency. Season with salt, cayenne pepper and paprika to taste. Chill, covered with plastic wrap for 2 hours.

Prepare cherry tomatoes by cutting off tops and using a teaspoon to scoop out centres. Invert onto absorbent paper to drain. Brush the rims of tomato shells with oil and dip into chopped parsley to coat. Pipe or spoon hummus into each case and drizzle a few drops of oil over the top. Garnish with reserved chick peas. This dish may be prepared ahead and stored, covered, in the refrigerator for 3 hours.

Makes about 30

VEGETABLE CRUDITES WITH TOMATO DIP

Tomato Dip
*¼ cup mayonnaise (see recipe)
300 mL sour cream (dairy
soured)
2 tablespoons natural yoghurt
3 tablespoons tomato paste
3 tablespoons tomato chutney
1 clove garlic, crushed
¼ teaspoon cayenne pepper
freshly ground black pepper*

Crudites
*2 carrots, peeled
3 sticks celery
4 zucchini
300 g broccoli, broken into
florets
125 g button mushrooms
250 g cherry tomatoes*

Combine the dip ingredients, mixing until well blended and smooth. Spoon into a serving dish, cover and chill until serving time.

To make the crudites, cut the carrots, celery and zucchini into matchsticks. Rinse the remaining ingredients in cold water. Place dip in the centre of a serving platter, surrounded with vegetables.

Serves 6

CAVIAR SNOW PEAS

As this dish is served chilled, the peas and topping can be prepared in advance. Choose snow peas that are approximately the same size.

300 g snow peas
250 g processed cream cheese
1 red capsicum, seeded and finely chopped
1 tablespoon chopped fresh dill
2 tablespoons chopped fresh parsley
freshly ground pepper
1 small jar red lumpfish roe

Blanch the snow peas in boiling water for 1 minute only. Drain and refresh under cold running water. Set aside.

Beat the cream cheese until softened. Stir through capsicum and herbs, and adjust seasoning to taste. Put mixture in a piping bag fitted with a 1 cm fluted tube. Arrange the snow peas attractively on a serving platter. Pipe rosettes along one side of each snow pea. Carefully spoon a little lumpfish roe on top of piped cream cheese. Chill until serving time. Serve as part of a selection of pre-dinner nibbles.

Serves 6

ITALIAN TOMATO APPETISERS

12 thick slices tomato
4 tablespoons Italian dressing (see recipe)
approximately 18 leaves fresh basil, finely chopped
12 slices mozzarella cheese

Place tomato slices in a shallow tray, sprinkle with dressing and top with half the basil leaves. Allow to rest, turning at least once, for a minimum of 2 hours.

When required place tomatoes on a foil-lined griller pan and top with cheese slices. Cook under a hot grill allowing cheese to melt over tomatoes. Pour over remaining dressing and basil and serve 2 slices per person.

Serves 6

WHOLEMEAL PASTA AND AVOCADO COCKTAIL

225 g wholemeal pasta shells
3 tablespoons oil
1 tablespoon wine vinegar
salt and freshly ground pepper
1 large ripe avocado
grated rind and juice 1 lemon
1 clove garlic, crushed
2 teaspoons sugar
4 shallots, sliced
1 tablespoon chopped parsley

Cook pasta shells in boiling, salted water until tender, then drain well. Blend oil with vinegar and a little seasoning, pour over drained pasta and toss lightly. Halve the avocado, scoop out the flesh and mash with lemon rind and juice, garlic and sugar. Stir in the shallots and parsley, then add pasta and stir lightly. Divide the mixture between 4 individual serving dishes and serve cold.

Serves 4

Left to right: Caviar Snow Peas, Italian Tomato Appetisers

Sasaki Calcutta plates

CAPONATA

Although Caponata is not, strictly speaking, a salad it makes a delicious first course as a cold vegetable dish, or part of a spread of vegetarian dishes.

500 g eggplants
salt
1 small onion, chopped
½ cup olive oil
3 stalks celery, diced
250 g tomatoes, peeled and chopped
12 green olives, stoned
1 tablespoon capers, drained
freshly ground black pepper
1 tablespoon sugar
2 tablespoons white wine vinegar

Cut eggplants into cubes, about 1.5 cm square. Make layers of the cubes in a colander, sprinkling each layer with salt. Weigh down with a plate and leave for 1 hour.

Fry onion in 2 tablespoons olive oil; when it starts to turn golden, add celery. After 2–3 minutes add tomatoes. Cook gently until thickened, about 10–15 minutes, adding olives, capers, black pepper, sugar and vinegar halfway through.

Rinse and dry eggplant, and heat remaining oil in a clean pan. Add eggplant and cook until golden, turning the cubes as they brown. When softened, remove from pan using a slotted spoon, leaving the oil in the pan, and mix eggplants with the other vegetables. Spoon into a shallow dish and leave to cool.

Serve at room temperature.

Serves 4–5

HERB CHEESE

250 g ricotta cheese
¼ cup snipped chives
½ bunch shallots, chopped
¼ cup chopped fresh mint
salt and freshly ground black pepper

Combine ricotta in a bowl with chives, shallots and mint. Season with salt and freshly ground pepper. Use as required.

Makes 2 cups

APPLE AND BEETROOT BOATS

3 uncooked beetroot
3 green apples
1 medium-sized Chinese radish
6 shallots, finely chopped
½ bunch chives, finely chopped
5 tablespoons vinaigrette, made with Dijon-style mustard (see recipe)
12 cos lettuce leaves
6 sprigs fresh basil or a few alfalfa sprouts, for decoration

Peel and wash beets. Grate on food processor or large holes on grater. Treat apples and radish in the same manner. Mix together in a bowl with shallots and chives.

Pour dressing over and allow to steep for at least ½ an hour before serving on 2 lettuce leaves per person — shaped into boats on individual plates. Decorate with a flag of basil or top with a pinch of alfalfa.

Serves 6

MELT IN THE MOUTH CHEESE SALAD

6 half-inch thick slices of Chevre (goats milk) cheese, well chilled
1 cup fresh breadcrumbs, lightly toasted in oven
60 g unsalted butter
1 iceberg lettuce, shredded
5 tablespoons vinaigrette, made with Dijon-style mustard (see recipe)

Cut chilled cheese with a sharp knife dipped first in boiling water to prevent cheese breaking. Place breadcrumbs in a plastic bag. Put each slice of cheese into bag individually and toss gently to cover with crumbs.

Melt butter over medium heat and fry gently but quickly on both sides until golden, using a spatula to turn. Have individual salad bowls ready and line with dressed, shredded lettuce. Top with melting cheese slices and serve with a crusty loaf.

Serves 6

FLORETS OF CAULIFLOWER IN JADE CLOAK

1 medium-sized cauliflower
almond slivers, to serve

Marinade
½ cup safflower oil
2 tablespoons lemon juice
salt and freshly ground pepper

Topping
2 ripe avocados
1 medium-sized onion, grated
2 tablespoons lemon juice
2 tablespoons finely chopped coriander leaves
¼ teaspoon salt
1 red radicchio or mignonette lettuce

Discarding thick base of cauliflower, cut off florets and steam until tender but still firm. Cover with marinade while still warm and allow to steep for at least 1 hour or cover and refrigerate overnight.

To serve, mash avocados with onion, lemon juice, coriander and salt. Shape 2 lettuce leaves into a nest per person on a small plate and fill with cauliflower florets. Coat with avocado topping and dust with almond slivers.

Serves 6–8

STUFFED VINE LEAVES

*250 g preserved vine leaves,
rinsed in hot water
juice ½ lemon
2 tablespoons olive oil*

Filling
*⅔ cup long-grain rice
1 tablespoon olive oil
1 large onion, finely chopped
2 tablespoons pine nuts
2 tablespoons chopped parsley
1 cup grated tasty cheese
2 tablespoons currants, washed
freshly ground pepper*

Lay the vine leaves flat on a work bench, shiny side down. Set aside any torn leaves.

To make the filling, wash rice well and drain. Heat oil and fry onion until soft. Add pine nuts and fry until just golden. Off the heat add rice and remaining ingredients. As the vine leaves are salty, no added salt is really necessary. Put a spoonful of filling onto a vine leaf. Fold over the end and sides and roll up. Repeat with remaining filling and leaves.

Line the base of a saucepan with the damaged leaves. Place stuffed leaf parcels on top, close together and seam side down. Cover with an inverted plate. Pour over lemon juice, olive oil and enough water to just cover the plate. Cover pan, bring to the boil, reduce heat and simmer for 40 minutes. Remove and taste a vine leaf — the rice should be tender. Cool in the liquid.

Remove plate. Arrange drained vine leaves on a serving plate and serve cool or chilled.

Makes approximately 40–45 vine leaves

STUFFED CELERY

*4 stalks celery
2 tablespoons sultanas
2 teaspoons dry sherry
185 g cottage cheese, sieved
60 g blue vein cheese, crumbled
2 gherkins, diced
1 tablespoon snipped chives*

Wash celery and cut off leaves and wide base section. Cut into 5 cm lengths and place in iced water for 15 minutes. Combine sultanas and sherry and leave for 15 minutes. Mix cheeses, gherkins, and chives. Beat well. Drain sultanas if necessary and stir into cheese mixture.

Drain celery and dry. Spoon or pipe cheese mixture into the hollow of the celery. Chill until serving time. To carry to a picnic, place in a lidded plastic container.

Serves 4–6

STUFFED NASTURTIUM LEAVES

If you have nasturtiums growing in your garden the leaves are edible. Pick the leaves and wash well — remembering to check for snails. The flowers can be used as a garnish for this unusual recipe. Nasturtium buds can be pickled and taste very similar to capers.

*24–30 nasturtium leaves, very
well washed
1 quantity herb cheese (see
recipe)
paprika, to taste
nasturtium flowers, to garnish
(optional)*

Shake the leaves dry. Spread a thick layer of herb cheese over one half of each leaf. Fold the other half of the leaf over and press lightly to seal. Do not completely close. Lightly sprinkle the exposed cheese with paprika. Chill and serve garnished with nasturtium flowers.

Serves 6–8, depending on the size of the leaves

PROSCIUTTO HAM WITH MELON

Smoked ham and sweet melon are perfect partners. Serve as an entree or part of a cold buffet.

*1 ripe melon, chilled
6–8 thin slices prosciutto (Parma)
ham*

Seed and cut melon into 6–8 slices. Serve each portion of melon with a slice of prosciutto draped over it.

Serves 6–8

**Clockwise: Prosciutto Ham with Melon,
Stuffed Nasturtium Leaves,
Stuffed Celery, Stuffed Vine Leaves**

EGGPLANT SHELLS WITH SAVOURY TOMATO FILLING

3 eggplants
chopped fresh parsley, to serve

Filling
1 garlic clove, crushed
2 onions, chopped
3 large tomatoes, peeled, seeded and chopped
2 tablespoons currants
3 tablespoons olive oil

Topping
½ cup oil
1 teaspoon sugar
salt
juice 1 lemon

Slice eggplants in half lengthways. Salt lightly and stand 30 minutes to drain. Rinse and wipe dry and scoop out centres. Use ½ shell for each person.

Saute filling ingredients including diced eggplant flesh in olive oil until onion is soft, then pile into the shells. Place in a baking dish and brush with combined topping ingredients.

Fill dish with water halfway up shells, then cover and simmer gently until soft. Arrange on a serving dish and chill for 24 hours. Serve sprinkled with chopped parsley.

Serves 6

AVOCADO AND PAW-PAW SALAD

2 ripe avocados, peeled, seeded and sliced
3 tablespoons fresh lime juice
1 medium-sized pawpaw, peeled, seeded and sliced
walnut dressing (see recipe [2])

Garnish
½ cup slivered almonds
4 cherry tomatoes
sprig fresh watercress

Sprinkle avocado slices with lime juice to prevent browning. Arrange pawpaw and avocado slices like a fan on chilled individual plates. Pour walnut dressing over fruit and garnish as suggested.

Serves 4

SMOKED TURKEY AND PAWPAW WITH CRANBERRY MAYONNAISE

1 medium-sized pawpaw, peeled, halved and seeded
12 thin slices smoked turkey breast
lime wedges and sprigs fresh watercress, to garnish

Cranberry Mayonnaise
6–8 tablespoons mayonnaise (see recipe) blended with
3 tablespoons cranberry sauce

Slice pawpaw. Arrange with 2 thin turkey slices. Place on individual plates, garnished with lime and watercress sprigs. Serve with cranberry mayonnaise.

Serves 6

SPINACH AND BACON SALAD

1 bunch small leaf English-style spinach
250 g button mushrooms, finely sliced
juice 1 lemon
4–6 rashers bacon, diced and rinds removed
2 tablespoons oil
3 cloves garlic, finely chopped
freshly ground pepper

Destalk and devein spinach, plunge into a bowl of iced water. Drain well and dry in a clean tea towel. Sprinkle mushrooms with lemon juice and set aside.

Fry bacon in oil with garlic until well browned and crisp. Tear spinach leaves into a salad bowl and sprinkle with mushrooms, bacon and garlic. Season with pepper, toss well and serve immediately.

Serves 4–6

Avocado and Pawpaw Salad

Sasaki plate

WARM CHICKEN LIVER SALAD

1 tablespoon oil
60 g unsalted butter
2 cloves garlic, finely chopped
500 g chicken livers, trimmed of threads but whole
12 shallots, each sliced into 4 pieces
12 miniature button mushrooms
4 tablespoons finely chopped parsley
juice 1 lemon
1 butter or radicchio lettuce
freshly ground pepper

Combine oil and butter over medium heat, add garlic and whole livers. Cook approximately 8 minutes until the livers are opaque — cooked but slightly tinged with pink on the inside. They should not be browned. Remove with a slotted spoon and keep warm.

Add shallots and mushrooms. Cook 1 minute, stirring continuously. Add parsley and lemon juice. Set aside and keep warm.

Place 2 lettuce leaves to form cups on individual plates. Fill with 2 or 3 livers. Spoon mushroom mixture over and sprinkle with pepper. If you like salt, do not add it until salad is assembled, as it toughens livers during cooking. Serve with toast triangles.

Serves 4–6

Warm Chicken Liver Salad

SALAD OF BRAINS SUPREME

6 sets brains
4 tablespoons vinaigrette (see recipe)
1 butter or radicchio lettuce
juice ½ lemon
1 tablespoon capers
freshly ground pepper

Rinse brains carefully so as not to break them and bring to the boil in lightly salted water. Lower heat and simmer for 5 minutes. Drain and place in a bowl and immediately cover with vinaigrette dressing. Allow to marinate for at least 2 hours, tossing occasionally.

When ready to serve, line individual bowls with lettuce leaves sprinkled with lemon juice. Centre whole or chopped brains, top with capers and sprinkle with pepper.

Serves 6

CRAYFISH CALYPSO

An excellent starter for a summer meal or sufficient for a light meal.

1 cos lettuce
1 mango
1 heaped teaspoon Madras curry powder
2 tablespoons mayonnaise (see recipe)
1 tablespoon cream
Balmain bugs, prawns, crabmeat, crayfish or a mixture of any or all
sprigs fresh dill

Discard outer leaves of lettuce. Rinse remainder and pat dry in clean tea towel. Allow to crisp in refrigerator. Peel, core and mash mango. Do not pulp totally.

Stir curry powder into mayonnaise and add cream. Mix in mango and chill for at least 1 hour under plastic wrap.

To serve, shape 2 lettuce leaves into a boat shape, fill with mango mixture and top with selected seafood. Decorate plate with a sprig of dill.

Serves 4

RAW FISH SALAD STARTER

500 g firm white fish fillets
1 cup lime juice
1 tablespoon hot pepper sauce or sambal oelek
1 white onion, finely chopped
1 large tomato, peeled, seeded and diced
½ cup olive oil
½ teaspoon salt
1 red capsicum, seeded and thinly sliced

Place fish fillets in a glass dish and pour over the next 6 ingredients. Cover and allow to rest about 1½–2 hours in refrigerator until fish turns opaque. Turn occasionally. When required remove skin from fish and break up flesh. Drain off most of the juice and place fish in individual bowls. Decorate with thin strips of capsicum and serve with a crusty hot loaf.

Serves 4–6

PRAWN SASHIMI

Prawn sashimi is a simple and splendid starter for a Japanese style dinner or a delicious appetiser to go with drinks.

12 uncooked king prawns
15 cm daikon
7 cm fresh ginger root
2 teaspoons wasabi paste
1 lemon, very thinly sliced
1 tablespoon very finely chopped
fresh parsley

Dipping Sauce
5 cm piece ginger root
½ cup Japanese soy sauce
1 tablespoon mirin or dry sherry

Prepare sauce by grating ginger and mixing with remaining ingredients. Set aside until required.

Peel the prawns leaving tails on each prawn. Make an incision along underside of each prawn but do not cut through the back. If necessary, devein and pat dry. On a flat surface make an incision roughly 1 cm from the head end to the tail and pull the head through the slit to form a butterfly shape.

Peel and shred both daikon and ginger and mix. Place a little on individual serving plates. Place 2 prawns per serving on each plate and a spot of wasabi paste along side. Garnish with a thin lemon slice sprinkled with finely chopped parsley.

Note: Daikon, wasabi paste and mirin wine are all Japanese ingredients which can be bought at Asian food stores.

Serves 6

BABY CALAMARI AND CELERY SALAD

1 kg baby calamari
1 teaspoon salt
juice ¼ lemon
1 bay leaf

Marinade
2–3 cloves garlic, minced with
1 teaspoon salt
5 tablespoons olive oil
juice 1 large lemon
freshly ground pepper

Celery Salad
½ bunch celery, chopped
2 tablespoons finely chopped
parsley
4 tablespoons vinaigrette (see
recipe)

Clean calamari under running water. Invert sac containing ink, cut off and discard. Bring calamari to the boil in a large pan with salt, lemon juice and bay leaf. Simmer for 20 minutes, drain well.

While simmering, combine marinade ingredients in a jar and shake well. Chop calamari into small pieces and top with marinade. Cover dish with plastic wrap and refrigerate overnight. Remove 1 hour before serving and toss well several times.

To serve, prepare celery salad then place 1 heaped tablespoon of each salad on individual plates. Accompany with a crusty loaf.

Serves 8

SCALLOPS AND CUCUMBER SALAD

6 cups water
500 g scallops
2 small cucumbers, scored and
cut into 24 rounds
16 inner leaves romaine lettuce
2 medium-sized tomatoes, sliced
bunch fresh chives, snipped
Spanish sherry wine vinegar
salt and freshly ground pepper

Bring water to gentle simmer in a large saucepan over medium heat. Add scallops and cook 3–5 seconds. Drain immediately and transfer to a bowl of iced water to stop cooking process. Drain again and set aside. (Can be prepared 1 day ahead to this point, covered and refrigerated.)

Combine ingredients and drizzle wine vinegar over all, sprinkle with salt and pepper to taste, and serve.

Serves 4

PRAWN AND CUCUMBER NESTS WITH DILL MAYONNAISE

1 long telegraph cucumber
1 punnet cherry tomatoes
1 bunch watercress
18 king prawns (3 per person)

Dill Mayonnaise
1 egg
1 tablespoon lemon juice
3 tablespoons olive oil
2 tablespoons finely chopped
fresh dill
freshly ground white pepper
salt

Peel cucumber with potato peeler, halve lengthways and scoop out seeds. Slice into julienne strips and crisp in iced water for 2 hours in refrigerator. Pour boiling water over tomatoes, pierce immediately, then peel. Refresh under cold water.

Prepare dressing by beating egg and lemon juice together, then slowly add oil to form a mayonnaise. Blend in dill and seasoning. Bought mayonnaise can be used instead if you do not have the time to prepare fresh; in which case fold dill into mayonnaise and mix with 1 tablespoon cream.

Wash and dry watercress, remove thicker stems and shape into nests on individal plates. Line with drained julienne cucumber. Pour over dill mayonnaise and top with prawns. Decorate with cherry tomatoes and serve.

Serves 6

From top: Baby Calamari and Celery Salad, Prawn and Cucumber Nests with Dill Mayonnaise, Scallops and Cucumber Salad

SALAD ON THE SIDE

You've planned your starters and a main course. Now you need a brilliant side salad. Something that sets the palate tingling with its freshness and flavour and complements the other dishes you have prepared. A side salad can be served American style with the main meal or in the European manner after the main course with cheese. Many dishes such as Greek Salad or Avocado and Watercress Salad are delicious and substantial enough to serve as a light lunch.

CAESAR SALAD

1 cos or butter lettuce
4 anchovy fillets
1 clove garlic, crushed
8 slices French bread
olive oil
1 egg, soft-boiled
salt and fresh ground black pepper
2 tablespoons lemon juice
1 teaspoon Worcestershire sauce
3 tablespoons Parmesan cheese freshly grated

Wash and dry lettuce. Tear into bite-sized pieces and leave to crisp in the refrigerator while preparing remaining ingredients. Mash anchovy fillets and mix with garlic. Spread mixture over bread slices and drizzle with a little oil. Bake at 150°C (300°F) for 25 minutes or until crisp. Allow to cool.

When ready to serve, place lettuce in a large bowl and top with bread. Roughly chop soft-boiled egg and add to lettuce with 3 tablespoons olive oil. Season to taste, pour over lemon juice and Worcestershire sauce, and sprinkle with Parmesan cheese. Toss well and serve at once.

Serves 4

CHEF'S SALAD

1 iceberg lettuce, washed and separated
3 hard-boiled eggs, shelled and chopped
125 g ham, cut in strips
4–6 rashers bacon, diced
3 shallots, sliced
¼ cup white wine vinegar
1 teaspoon caster sugar
salt and freshly ground pepper
Worcestershire sauce
2 tablespoons chopped olives

Place lettuce leaves in salad bowl. Arrange egg and ham on lettuce. Cook bacon until crisp. Remove and set aside, saving bacon dripping.

Saute shallots in dripping. Add vinegar, sugar, salt and pepper and Worcestershire sauce. Pour hot dressing over lettuce. Crumble bacon on top, sprinkle with chopped olives and toss.

Serves 6

AVOCADO AND WATERCRESS SALAD

4 ripe avocados, peeled, seeded and diced
1 cup button mushrooms, sliced
2 cups watercress, firmly packed
1 onion, finely chopped
2 cloves garlic, crushed
½ cup chopped fresh parsley
salt and freshly ground pepper
juice 1 lemon
2 tablespoons olive oil

Watercress and Yoghurt Dressing
2 cups unflavoured yoghurt
2 cups watercress leaves, firmly packed
1 tablespoon grated onion
½ teaspoon mustard
pinch cayenne pepper
salt

In a bowl combine all ingredients. Carefully toss mixture.

To make dressing, place all ingredients in a small bowl and beat until well combined. Chill for at least 1 hour before serving with avocados.

Serves 4

GREEN SALAD

1 lettuce, core removed
4 shallots, sliced
½ cucumber, peeled, seeded and
sliced
pinch salt
1 clove garlic, peeled
1 tablespoon chopped fresh
parsley
2 tablespoons olive oil
freshly ground black pepper
2 tablespoons white wine vinegar

Rinse salad greens quickly under cold running water. Shake off excess water then pat dry with absorbent paper. Place in a plastic bag and chill in the refrigerator. Just before making the salad, tear lettuce into bite-sized pieces.

Rub a salad bowl with salt and garlic, extracting as much juice as possible from the garlic. Discard garlic clove.

Combine salad greens and herbs in bowl. Sprinkle over olive oil and toss salad until all the leaves are coated. Add black pepper to taste. Sprinkle over vinegar and serve.

Serves 4

SESAME SPINACH SALAD

1 bunch small leaf English-style
spinach
3 tablespoons sesame seeds
3 tablespoons olive oil
1 tablespoon lemon juice
1 teaspoon soy sauce
dash hot pepper sauce (eg
Tabasco)
260 g can water chestnuts,
drained and sliced
8 button mushrooms, sliced

Stem and devein spinach leaves, rinse in cold water and dry in clean tea towel. Place in refrigerator in tea towel to crisp. Toast sesame seeds in a frypan over moderate heat, shaking constantly to prevent burning. Cool seeds. Combine the next 4 ingredients in a glass jar and shake well.

To serve, tear spinach leaves into salad bowl, coat with dressing, then fold in water chestnuts and mushrooms. Dust with toasted sesame seeds.

Serves 6

GREEK SALAD

Often served in restaurants, Greek Salad offers a delicious combination of flavours. One cannot resist picking at the salad before the accompanying meal reaches the table.

Salad
1 iceberg lettuce, washed and
separated
4 ripe tomatoes, cut into wedges
4 shallots, finely chopped
1 onion, thinly sliced
1 green capsicum, seeded and
sliced
12 large black olives
100 g feta cheese, diced

Dressing
3 tablespoons olive oil
1 tablespoon lemon juice
pinch dried oregano
salt and freshly ground black
pepper

Tear lettuce leaves into bite-sized pieces. Mix with remaining ingredients in a salad bowl and toss gently. Combine all dressing ingredients in a jar and shake until well blended. Just before serving, sprinkle dressing over the salad.

Serves 6

WALDORF SALAD

6 tart red apples, diced with skin
retained
2 tablespoons lemon juice
1½ cups sliced celery
90 g walnuts, coarsely chopped
1½ cups mayonnaise (see recipe)
1 medium-sized lettuce

Sprinkle unpeeled diced apple with lemon juice. Combine in a salad bowl with celery, nuts and mayonnaise, stirring until well combined.

Serves 6

Venezia plate

Greek Salad

Venezia plate

Warm Cherry Tomato Salad

WARM CHERRY TOMATO SALAD

2 tablespoons olive oil
2 tablespoons raw sugar
1 tablespoon chopped fresh oregano or ½ teaspoon dried
4 spring onions, thinly sliced
2 punnets cherry tomatoes
3 tablespoons vinaigrette (see recipe)
3 tablespoons finely chopped fresh basil

Heat oil over medium heat, stir in sugar and oregano. Add onion slices and increase heat slightly to colour onion, stirring constantly to prevent sticking. Lower heat as soon as coloured and add tomatoes, taking care that skins do not burst. Stir gently for about 2 minutes then remove to serving dish with slotted spoon. Sprinkle with dressing and dust with basil.

Serves 4–6

CHERRY TOMATOES WITH BASIL

1 punnet cherry tomatoes, washed
250 g ricotta cheese
⅓ cup grated fresh Parmesan cheese
3–4 tablespoons chopped fresh basil
freshly ground pepper
2 tablespoons snipped chives

Cut a slice from top of tomatoes. With the handle of a teaspoon scoop out the seeds and membrane. Stand inverted to drain for 20 minutes.

Combine cheeses and basil with freshly ground pepper to taste. Place mixture in a piping bag fitted with a 1 cm plain nozzle. Carefully pipe some cheese mixture into each tomato. Chill until serving time.

To carry to a picnic, place in a lidded plastic container. Just before serving, sprinkle with chives.

Serves 6–8

TOMATO AND BASIL SALAD

500 g firm ripe tomatoes, thinly sliced
grated rind and juice 1 small lemon
salt and freshly ground pepper
3 tablespoons olive oil
pinch sugar
3 shallots, finely sliced
1 tablespoon chopped fresh basil

Arrange tomato slices in a shallow serving dish, sprinkle with lemon rind and season with salt.

Beat 1 tablespoon lemon juice with the oil and season with salt, pepper and sugar. Scatter shallots and basil over tomatoes and sprinkle over dressing. Leave for 1 hour before serving.

Serves 4–6

35

Supreme Asparagus Salad

SUPREME ASPARAGUS SALAD

4 bunches asparagus
1 teaspoon salt
*1 bunch watercress, thickest
stems removed, remaining finely
chopped*
4 tablespoons sour cream
2 tablespoons lemon juice
½ bunch chives, finely chopped
freshly ground white pepper

Should you have a saucepan large enough to allow asparagus to stand up in it, so much the better, as this is the best method to prevent the tips from breaking. Otherwise lie asparagus in a shallow pan (in separate batches if necessary) and pour boiling water over it. Add salt and allow to simmer for no more than 15 minutes. Drain and immediately plunge into iced water to refresh. This is essential for the retention of both colour and texture. Cover and keep in refrigerator until required. It is best consumed within hours.

Mix remaining ingredients in a bowl when you are ready to serve and either place the asparagus in individual plates with the dressing as a topping, or place asparagus on a decorative platter and pour the topping over.

Serves 4–6

Tableware — Lifestyle Imports

SWEET POTATO SALAD

2 orange sweet potatoes
juice 1 large orange
juice ½ lemon
1 tablespoon honey
1 tablespoon preserved ginger,
drained and finely chopped
2 tablespoons sesame seeds,
lightly toasted

Peel potatoes, halve and steam over boiling water until tender but firm. Allow to cool, then slice. Bring orange and lemon juices and honey to the boil, cool slightly and pour over sliced potatoes. Add chopped ginger, cover and place in refrigerator for at least 1 hour. Serve potato salad dusted with sesame seeds.

Serves 6

ZUCCHINI SALAD

6 zucchini, very thinly sliced
2 tablespoons white wine vinegar
1 green capsicum, finely
shredded
2 stalks celery, finely sliced
½ large white onion, grated
1 tablespoon sugar
½ cup olive oil
1 tablespoon red wine vinegar
2 tablespoons red wine
1 teaspoon salt

If you have a food processor this salad can be prepared in minutes and will keep for a week. Prepare all ingredients and combine in a bowl. Preferably allow the mixture to mature overnight before serving.

Serves 4–6

Carrot Salad

CARROT SALAD

4 carrots, peeled and sliced
2 oranges, segmented
1 pear, diced
2 tablespoons lemon juice
90 g cream cheese
¼ cup cream
salt and freshly ground pepper

Place carrots and oranges in a bowl. Mix pear with 1 tablespoon lemon juice and add to the bowl. Mix remaining lemon juice with the cream cheese and whisk until thick. Fold cream into cream cheese mixture, season with salt and pepper. Drizzle over the carrot mixture and serve chilled.

Serves 4

CARROT AND APPLE SALAD

3 large carrots, grated
3 apples, grated
2 tablespoons lemon juice
1 tablespoon poppy seeds

Combine all ingredients, toss lightly and chill to serve. This is excellent with fish dishes.

Serves 6

EGGS NEST

4 eggs
1 bunch small leaf English-style spinach
4 rashers bacon, diced and rinds removed
1–2 cloves garlic, crushed
3 slices bread, diced
6 button mushrooms, sliced
juice 1 lemon
440 g can corn kernels, drained

Soft-boil eggs for 4 minutes and cool under cold water. Tap shells but do not peel until required. (This ensures that shells will not adhere to eggs and thus break them.) Wash and devein spinach. Dry and chill in refrigerator to crisp.

Fry bacon with garlic. Remove with slotted spoon, drain on kitchen paper and keep warm. Fry croutons in bacon fat. Add a little oil if necessary, and toss to prevent burning.

Tear spinach into bite-sized pieces and place in salad bowl. Sprinkle mushroom slices with lemon juice and fold in. Add corn, bacon, croutons and remaining bacon fat. Toss well.

Serve in individual salad bowls topped with peeled egg per serve. The eggs should be just runny when pierced.

Serves 4

SLICED POTATOES VINAIGRETTE

Small red new potatoes are perfect for this salad. Chilling them slightly in water makes for neat slices.

1 kg small red new potatoes, unpeeled
½ cup chopped fresh parsley
¼ cup freshly snipped chives
¾ cup safflower oil
¼ cup red wine vinegar
2 teaspoons dry mustard
1 teaspoon salt
freshly ground pepper

Cook potatoes until they can be pierced through with a sharp knife (do not overcook). Drain and cover with cold water. Let stand 12 minutes and drain again.

Combine finely chopped parsley and chives in a bowl. Add oil, vinegar and seasoning and whisk to blend. Leave vinaigrette in a bowl.

Slice potatoes into vinaigrette. Invert mixture into serving bowl. Toss gently to coat potatoes evenly, adjust seasoning and serve at room temperature.

Serves 8

SICILIAN FENNEL SALAD

1 clove garlic, crushed
1 cucumber, peeled and sliced
1 onion, sliced
1 orange, peeled and sliced
4 tomatoes, sliced
1 bulb fennel, grated

Dressing
1 tablespoon oil
2 tablespoons lemon juice
½ teaspoon chopped fresh basil
freshly ground black pepper

Sprinkle garlic over salad platter. Layer vegetables and fruit on platter and chill. Shake dressing in jar, pour over salad and toss lightly.

Serves 4

BROCCOLI SALAD

3 large heads broccoli, thick stems discarded
Italian dressing (see recipe)

Lime Mayonnaise
2 cups mayonnaise (see recipe)
2 cups light sour cream
⅓ cup lime juice
1 tablespoon finely grated lime peel
2 tablespoons horseradish
1 tablespoon Dijon-style mustard

Pare bases of broccoli stems, place florets in a steamer and steam over boiling water until just tender (approximately 3 minutes). If you have only a small steamer this can be done in batches. When cooked, plunge instantly into iced water, taking care not to break the florets. Cool, cover with plastic wrap and refrigerate overnight.

When required to serve, sprinkle with Italian dressing (see recipe) and serve with lime mayonnaise. To make lime mayonnaise, whisk ingredients together in a bowl. This dressing can be prepared in advance and stored in the refrigerator.

Serves 8–10

CAULIFLOWER SALAD

1 medium-sized cauliflower
½ lemon
¼ cup vinegar
1 cup safflower oil
½ cup chopped fresh mint leaves
2 cups low calorie yoghurt

Cut florets from stem and discard core. Place in a saucepan with lemon and cover with boiling water. Lemon will keep cauliflower white. Cook for 3 minutes. Drain in colander and refresh under cold water for 1 minute, taking care to keep florets in shape.

Place in salad bowl, sprinkle with vinegar and oil. Dust with half the mint leaves and allow to rest for at least 25 minutes.

To serve, coat lightly with yoghurt and dust with remaining mint leaves. This salad is excellent with cold meats or chicken.

Serves 4–6

Broccoli Salad

GINGERED GREEN BEANS

1 cm piece ginger root, finely grated
1 teaspoon ground fenugreek
500 g green beans, trimmed and diagonally sliced
2 tablespoons finely chopped fresh mint
1 teaspoon olive oil

Pour enough water into a saucepan to cover the bottom and heat. Add ginger and fenugreek and cook for 2 minutes. Add beans and mint and toss lightly. Cook over low heat until beans are just tender. Remove from saucepan and refrigerate until chilled. Toss in olive oil before serving.

Serves 6

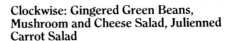
Clockwise: Gingered Green Beans, Mushroom and Cheese Salad, Julienned Carrot Salad

MUSHROOM AND CHEESE SALAD

250 g button mushrooms, trimmed
1 clove garlic, very finely chopped
1 small red capsicum, sliced
½ cup vinaigrette (see recipe)
125 g Edam cheese, diced

Combine all ingredients and leave to marinate for 30 minutes. Pour off the excess dressing. Serve chilled with crusty bread.

Serves 4

JULIENNED CARROT SALAD

Parboiling the carrots intensifies colour and natural sweetness. Cool carrots so they do not become too soft.

1 kg carrots, trimmed and cut into 2.5 cm julienne pieces
3 shallots
¼ cup lemon juice
¼ cup oil
1¼ teaspoons salt
1 teaspoon sugar
pinch cinnamon
pinch ground allspice
freshly ground black pepper
1 lettuce, cored and separated, to serve

Bring a large saucepan of salted water to boil over high heat. Add carrots and boil just until tender. Drain carrots well then rinse with cold water until carrots are completely cooled. Drain thoroughly and drain dry with absorbent paper.

Combine remaining ingredients in a jar and shake well or whisk in a bowl. Sprinkle dressing over the carrots, turning to coat. Arrange lettuce leaves in a salad bowl. Spoon carrots into the centre and serve.

Serves 6

SALAD SENSATIONS

*You don't have to be on a diet to enjoy salad as a main course
but there's no denying, these mouth-watering recipes will definitely help
the waistline keep its shape. There are salads that have seafood such as
tuna and salmon as their base, ones that combine fruit and cheese and
others that do wonders with spinach, nuts and potato. Looking for a taste
sensation? Try the Mediterranean Salad with its great combination of
eggplant, tomatoes and pasta flavoured with garlic and oregano.*

MEDITERRANEAN SALAD

1 large eggplant, cut into wedges
2 teaspoons salt
3 tablespoons oil
2 tablespoons safflower oil
2 cloves garlic
1 large onion, sliced thinly
*2 large tomatoes, peeled and
quartered*
¼–½ cup finely chopped parsley
2 tablespoons red wine vinegar
1 teaspoon dried oregano leaves
freshly ground pepper
500 g yellow pasta (carrot)

Sprinkle eggplant with salt and allow to
stand under heavy plate for 20 minutes.
Rinse and pat dry with paper towels.
Heat half the two oils (combined) over
medium heat in a large pan, add garlic
and onion and cook until softened but
not browned. Add half the eggplant
slices and cook until tender shaking the
pan to prevent sticking. Remove with
slotted spoon onto a warm plate, then
cook remaining eggplant. When tender,
add tomatoes and remaining ingredients,
stirring gently.

Stir in all the eggplant and keep warm.
Cook pasta *al dente* and when well
drained add vegetable mixture. Serve
tepid.

Serves 8

SPINACH AND PECAN SALAD

If English-style spinach is unavailable,
silverbeet can be substituted but it has a
stronger 'metallic' flavour. If carrying this
salad to a picnic, carry the dressing in a
jar and the remaining ingredients in a
plastic bag. To serve, simply tip the
dressing into the bag, seal and shake the
bag to coat the salad with the dressing.

1 bunch English-style spinach
6 slices French bread
2 cloves garlic, peeled
1 tablespoon olive oil
*100 g pecan nuts, roughly
chopped*
60 g smoked cheese, diced
60 g Edam cheese, diced
1 tablespoon chopped mint
½ cup vinaigrette (see recipe)

Wash and dry the spinach. Cut off the
stalks and tear the leaves into pieces.
Rub each side of the bread with the garlic. Sprinkle the bread with the olive oil
then cut into small pieces. Fry the bread
in a dry pan until golden. Cool.

Combine the spinach, bread, pecan
nuts, cheeses and mint. Pour over the
dressing and lightly toss, making sure all
spinach leaves are coated.

Serves 6–8

SMOKED SALMON WITH PICKLED PEACHES

*1 bunch watercress or endive
lettuce*
6 peaches
*2 tablespoons raspberry or red
wine vinegar*
2 tablespoons olive oil
freshly ground pepper
6 slices smoked salmon
1 tablespoon pink peppercorns

Wash and dry watercress, discarding
thicker stems, or tear endive into bite-
sized pieces. Allow to rest in refrigerator
to crisp until required. Pour boiling
water over peaches placed in a bowl.
Prick skin and peel. When cool, cut into
halves and sprinkle with vinegar.

When required, arrange watercress in
a salad bowl. Toss with oil and sprinkle
with pepper. Fold in pickled peaches and
decorate top of salad with rolls of
smoked salmon. (Wrap each slice of
salmon round the handle of a lightly
oiled wooden spoon and then slide off.)
Sprinkle with pink peppercorns.

Serves 6

SALA DI LUCCA

1 punnet cherry tomatoes
12 large black olives, drained,
pitted and halved
3 tablespoons finely chopped
fresh basil
2 tablespoons olive oil
juice ½ lemon
2 teaspoons chopped fresh
oregano leaves or ½ teaspoon
dried oregano
freshly ground pepper
1 small can anchovy fillets,
roughly chopped
500 g tagliatelle (flat pasta)

Dressing
1 clove garlic, crushed with ½
teaspoon salt
½ cup chopped parsley
6 spring onions, thinly sliced (not
shallots)
3 tablespoons olive oil

Combine all salad ingredients except pasta and mix well. Cook pasta *al dente*, place in colander and allow hot tap water to run through pasta briefly before draining well. Immediately place in a warmed serving dish and cover with dressing.

To make dressing, combine garlic, salt, parsley, spring onions and olive oil in a food processor or mix well by shaking in a screw-top jar.

Serves 6

GRUYERE AND GRAPE SALAD

185 g gruyere, cut in matchsticks
2 small radicchio lettuces,
washed and dried
½ bunch shallots, sliced
2 red apples, chopped
500 g seedless grapes
½ cup pecan nuts
½ cup vinaigrette (see recipe)
made with
walnut or hazelnut oil
½ bunch chives, snipped

Toss salad ingredients together in a bowl with dressing just before serving. Snip over chives and serve.

Serves 6

Arzberg plate

Pecan and Avocado Salad

PECAN AND AVOCADO SALAD

1 cos lettuce
5 tablespoons vinaigrette (see
recipe) prepared with walnut oil
and Dijon-style mustard
3 avocados
lemon juice
4 tablespoons pecan nuts

Tear rinsed and dried lettuce into a salad bowl and coat with vinaigrette dressing. Peel, core and slice avocados and sprinkle with lemon juice to prevent browning. Fold nuts through salad and toss well. Add avocado and serve.

Serves 12

RED ROBINS' NEST

6 quail eggs or 3 hen eggs,
all hard-boiled, shelled
and quartered
1 red radicchio lettuce
1 plump whitloof, petalled
4 sticks celery, chopped
2 large carrots, grated
4 tablespoons mung beans
1 punnet cherry tomatoes
5 tablespoons vinaigrette made
with Dijon-style mustard (see
recipe)

Prepare eggs and set aside to cool. Wash and dry lettuce and whitloof and allow to crisp wrapped in a tea towel in the refrigerator until required. Mix the next 4 ingredients in a separate bowl and toss well with vinaigrette.

Allow to steep for at least ½ hour. To serve, line a salad bowl alternately with leaves of red radicchio and whitloof. Fill the centre with mixed vegetables and top with quail eggs. This salad is excellent with smoked chicken or ham.

Serves 6

Red Robin's Nest

SUNBURST SALAD

1 bunch English-style spinach
2 whitloof hearts
juice ½ lemon
2 ripe avocados, peeled and
sliced into half rings
3 rashers bacon, rind removed
and diced
2 slices bread, diced
1 can sliced water chestnuts,
drained

Dressing
4 tablespoons vinaigrette (see
recipe) prepared with Meaux
mustard, or use mustard and
coarsely ground pepper

Prepare dressing and set aside. Cut roots from spinach and devein. Rinse under cold running water, drain and tear into bite-sized pieces. Place in a tea towel in refrigerator and allow to crisp.

Separate whitloof leaves and sprinkle with lemon juice to prevent discolouration. Place avocado on a plate and sprinkle lightly with lemon juice. Fry bacon until crisp. Remove, drain on kitchen paper and keep warm. Use bacon fat to fry bread croutons, turning frequently until golden.

On individual plates provide a bed of spinach per serve. Arrange whitloof leaves over spinach in a flower pattern. Sprinkle with water chestnuts and decorate centre with avocado rings. Pour dressing over and top with bacon and croutons to serve.

Serves 6

CREAMY SMOKED EEL SALAD

250 g smoked eel
250 g potatoes, cooked, peeled
and diced
2 heads Belgian endive (whitloof)
1 tablespoon snipped chives
6 radishes, sliced
walnut halves, to garnish

Dressing
grated rind and juice 1 large
lemon
100 mL sour cream
Tabasco sauce, to taste
1–2 tablespoons grated
horseradish

Prepare dressing first. Combine all ingredients. Taste and adjust seasoning and chill until ready to use.

Remove skin from eel and slice meat off the bone into bite-sized pieces. Place eel, potatoes, endive, chives and radishes in a bowl. Pour over the dressing and toss lightly but thoroughly. Serve garnished with walnuts.

Variation
If smoked eel is unavailable from your delicatessen, substitute smoked trout garnished with a little smoked salmon and sprigs of dill.

Serves 4

CHILLED MUSSEL SALAD

2 kg mussels, in shells
1 cup wine
1 cup water
few sprigs fresh parsley
3 bay leaves
1 teaspoon black peppercorns

Dressing
¼ cup white wine vinegar
salt and freshly ground pepper
1 teaspoon French mustard
¾ cup oil
4 hard-boiled eggs, chopped
¼ cup chopped fresh parsley
¾ teaspoon chopped fresh
tarragon
1 teaspoon snipped chives
2 teaspoons gherkins, chopped

Prepare the mussels for cooking by scrubbing them well and discarding any with open shells. Remove the 'beard' with a vegetable knife.

Bring the wine, water, parsley, bay leaves and peppercorns to the boil in a large pan then lower heat and simmer for 5 minutes. Add the mussels, cover and simmer until they open, about 3–5 minutes. Now remove the mussels and twist off the top shell, pouring off any cooking liquid. Arrange mussels in individual serving dishes discarding any that do not open.

To make the dressing, whisk vinegar, salt, pepper and mustard well to combine. Gradually add the oil, whisking constantly. Taste and adjust the seasoning. Add remaining ingredients, stirring to combine. Leave for 30 minutes for the flavours to blend and develop. Stir again then pour over the mussels.

Toss lightly so that all the mussels are coated with the dressing, then chill until serving time. Chilled mussel salad is delicious served with crusty bread and lemon wedges.

Serves 4–6

SKEWERED CORIANDER SEAFOOD SALAD

Skewers
1 kg firm white fish fillets
2 teaspoons finely grated ginger
root
3 cloves garlic, crushed
3 teaspoons ground coriander
1 teaspoon garam masala
½ teaspoon chilli powder
3 tablespoons lemon juice
1 cup yoghurt
2 tablespoons flour

Salad
2 carrots
2 cucumbers
10 snow peas
1 red capsicum, seeded

Cut the fish into 2.5 cm cubes and place in a shallow glass dish. Combine the remaining skewer ingredients mixing until smooth and pour over the fish. Cover and refrigerate for 30 minutes.

Preheat griller and thread fish pieces onto bamboo skewers — 4 or 5 pieces on each skewer. Place under griller and cook, turning occasionally for about 10 minutes or until the fish is starting to flake.

Using a sharp knife slice all the salad vegetables into fine julienne strips. Toss vegetables together to combine, then place on a serving dish. Arrange seafood skewers over the salad and serve at room temperature.

Serves 6

**Top: Chilled Mussel Salad
Bottom: Skewered Coriander Seafood Salad**

Sasaki plates

TUNA SALAD WITH GARLIC TOAST

*1 eggplant
salt and freshly ground pepper
2 tablespoons oil
3 tablespoons olive oil
1 tablespoon vinegar
½ teaspoon prepared French
mustard
225 g tuna in oil
2 sticks celery, chopped
8 black olives
1 long stick French bread
150 g butter
1–2 cloves garlic, chopped*

Peel eggplant, dice and sprinkle with salt; leave for 30 minutes. Wash well, pat dry and fry quickly in hot oil. Drain well and cool. Make a dressing from olive oil, vinegar and mustard.

Drain tuna well and place in a bowl with celery and eggplant. Pour over dressing and toss lightly. Garnish with olives and chill.

Slice bread. Combine butter and garlic then coat each piece of bread. Place on a baking sheet and bake at 190°C (375°F) for 10 minutes, or until crisp and brown. Serve immediately with tuna salad.

Serves 4

JANSSON'S TEMPTATION

*6 potatoes
3 onions, cut into rings
50 g butter
60 g can anchovy fillets, drained
and chopped
1 egg yolk
1 tablespoon flour
250 mL cream
extra 30 g butter*

Peel potatoes and cut into strips 1 cm wide. Cook onions in butter until soft, about 10 minutes.

In a greased casserole dish arrange layers of potatoes, onions and anchovies, starting and finishing with potatoes. Mix egg yolk and flour together. Add to cream and carefully pour mixture over potatoes and dot with extra butter.

Bake uncovered at 180°C (350°F) for 45–50 minutes or until potatoes are tender. Serve with a simple salad.

Serves 4–6

PRAWN AND TOMATO SHELLS

*8 even-sized ripe tomatoes
1 teaspoon gelatine
1 tablespoon water
½ cup mayonnaise (see recipe)
½ tablespoon lemon juice
dash Angostura bitters
250 g medium-sized cooked
prawns, shelled and deveined
1 tablespoon chopped fresh dill
watercress, to garnish*

Skin the tomatoes by first removing the core then plunging the tomatoes into boiling water for 2 minutes. The skin should peel away easily. Slice off the tops and reserve, scoop out the seeds and drain the shells upside down.

Dissolve gelatine in water and combine with mayonnaise, lemon juice and bitters. Leave to thicken slightly. Coat prawns with dressing and sprinkle with chopped dill.

Fill shells with prawns and top with the caps. Arrange the tomatoes on a platter and garnish with watercress.

Serves 8

PICKLED FISH WITH GREEN SALAD

*1 kg fish fillets, skinned
salt and freshly ground pepper
5 tablespoons oil
4 onions, sliced
2 medium-sized carrots, sliced
2 green capsicums, seeded and
sliced
2 bay leaves
1 clove garlic, crushed
2 whole red chillies
100 mL white wine vinegar
450 mL water*

Season fish fillets with salt and pepper. Heat 3 tablespoons oil in frypan and fry fish, in batches, until golden on both sides. Drain and place in shallow, heat-proof serving dish.

Place remaining ingredients and oil in frypan and season with ground pepper. Bring to the boil, reduce heat and simmer, covered, for 25 minutes or until vegetables are tender. Pour hot vinegar mixture over fish and leave to cool to room temperature. Chill before serving with a simple salad.

Serves 6

YABBIE MANGO SALAD WITH WALNUT HERB DRESSING

In days gone by one would have to go to great lengths to find yabbies living under rocks in cool, freshwater streams. These days, most seafood stores sell these tempting crustaceans still alive only a few hours after being plucked from a commercial farm dam. For those without access to this delicious seafood, scampi, canned crab, crayfish or prawns can be substituted.

*8 medium-sized yabbies or
scampi*

Dressing
*¼ cup walnut oil
2 tablespoons vinegar
1 tablespoon finely chopped
fresh chives
1½ tablespoons finely chopped
parsley
1 teaspoon capers, finely
chopped
freshly ground black pepper
1 ripe mango, peeled and finely
sliced
1 mignonette lettuce or radicchio,
well washed and separated into
leaves*

If yabbies are still alive, place in the freezer for approximately one hour. This kills them painlessly and minimises toughness when cooked. Bring a large saucepan of salted water to the boil. Add the yabbies and boil for 8 minutes. Drain and rinse under cold water.

Combine the dressing ingredients in a screw-top jar and shake until well blended. Using a large sharp knife, cut through yabbies lengthways, along the back. Open out and sprinkle with a little dressing.

Arrange mango and lettuce in a salad bowl. Place yabbies on top. Sprinkle over any remaining dressing and serve.

Serves 6

**Top: Yabbie Mango Salad with Walnut Herb
Dressing
Bottom: Pickled Fish with Green Salad**

PASTA SALAD WITH PESTO DRESSING

Pesto is an Italian sauce flavoured with basil and Parmesan cheese. Once made, the dressing can be kept refrigerated for up to 3 months. Use to add flavour to vegetables, poached fish or baby potatoes.

> *350 g green tagliatelle noodles*
> *1 cup mustard cress*
> *200 g cherry tomatoes*
> *4 slices leg ham, diced*

> ### Dressing
> *1 clove garlic, crushed*
> *¼ cup finely chopped fresh basil*
> *1 tablespoon grated Parmesan cheese*
> *¼ cup ground pine nuts or walnuts*
> *¼ cup olive oil*
> *3 tablespoons white wine or tarragon vinegar*

Cook pasta in 4 litres boiling salted water for 10–12 minutes until pasta is *al dente*. Adding 1 tablespoon oil to the water will prevent pasta from sticking or boiling over. Drain well and rinse in cold water and drain again.

Place pasta in salad bowl with remaining salad ingredients. Put all dressing ingredients in a large screw-top jar and shake well to combine. Sprinkle over the salad and toss before serving.

Serves 4

Venezia plates

Left to right: Pasta Salad with Pesto
Dressing, Farfalle and Spicy Tuna Salad,
Cold Pasta with Gazpacho

COLD PASTA WITH GAZPACHO

500 g spiralli pasta
2 green capsicum, seeded and
chopped
1 Spanish onion, chopped
6 shallots, thinly sliced
1 cup black olives, stoned and
sliced
1 cup finely chopped Italian
parsley
1 cup chopped fresh mint

Gazpacho dressing
½ cup olive oil
½ cup red wine vinegar
½ teaspoon ground cumin
2 cloves garlic, crushed
5 medium-sized tomatoes, peeled,
seeded and chopped
1 large cucumber, peeled, seeded
and chopped
salt and freshly ground black
pepper
1 teaspoon chilli sauce

Cook the pasta in 3 litres boiling
water until tender, about 10–12 minutes.
Drain well and place in a large bowl. To
make the dressing, combine all ingredients in a food processor and blend until
smooth.

Toss dressing through hot pasta.
Allow to cool to room temperature, stirring occasionally. Serve with remaining
ingredients tossed through pasta.

Serves 10–12

FARFALLE AND SPICY TUNA SALAD

500 g Farfalle (bow-shaped
pasta)
4 tablespoons vinaigrette (see
recipe)
185 g can tuna in oil
2 tablespoons capers
1 red capsicum, seeded and diced
8–12 fresh basil leaves, chopped
1 punnet cherry tomatoes or
small yellow equivalent
12 shallots, finely sliced

Cook pasta in boiling water for 12 minutes adding 1 tablespoon oil to prevent
pasta sticking together. Stir occasionally.
Drain and turn out into serving bowl.
Immediately cover with dressing, then
add tuna and toss well. Add all remaining
ingredients and serve with a crusty loaf.

Serves 6–8

HIGH-RISE SALAD

5 tablespoons walnut dressing
(see recipe [1])
1 butter lettuce, washed and
separated
440 g can asparagus tips,
drained
juice ½ lemon
4 zucchini, thinly sliced
3 artichoke hearts, halved
squeeze lemon juice
freshly ground pepper
6 slices rare cold roast beef,
thinly sliced
400 g can sweet pimiento,
drained
2 gherkins, thinly sliced
alfalfa sprouts or fresh basil
sprigs

Prepare dressing, allowing to mature for at least 1 hour. Place whole lettuce leaves in a bowl and pour over 3 tablespoons dressing. Place asparagus on a plate and sprinkle with lemon juice.

Blanch zucchini for 1 minute in boiling water, drain and cover with 1 tablespoon dressing. Sprinkle artichoke hearts with lemon juice and pepper. Leave all vegetables for 30 minutes.

To assemble salad arrange lettuce on individual plates and cover with roast beef. Top beef (enhance with a smidgeon of horseradish for extra flavour) with pimiento slice and stack on top all remaining ingredients.

Serves 6

TURKEY IN PINEAPPLE BOATS

2 medium-sized pineapples
4 sticks celery, thinly sliced
small bunch grapes, washed and
halved
2 tablespoons finely chopped
fresh mint
1 cold cooked turkey drumstick
or left-over meat
4 tablespoons mayonnaise (see
recipe)
2 tablespoons fresh cream
1 tablespoon horseradish
4 sprigs fresh mint
2 tablespoons slivered almonds,
toasted

Leaving the leaves on and using a sharp knife, halve pineapples and cut out centre flesh. Discard core, dice fruit and place in a bowl.

In a bowl, combine celery, grapes and mint. Cut poultry into julienne strips and add to fruit. Blend mayonnaise with cream and horseradish. Pour over fruit, cover and chill.

To serve, fill pineapples with mixture and decorate with mint and almonds. Replace tops and serve.
Note: This can be taken on a picnic and assembled on site.

Serves 4

CHICKEN AND ROCK MELON SALAD

2 chicken breasts
2 chicken stock cubes
3 tablespoons mayonnaise (see
recipe)
2 tablespoons light sour cream
1 red apple, cored, diced and
skin retained
juice ½ lemon
2 stalks celery, thinly sliced
4 tablespoons green grapes
2 or 3 rock melons, chilled
alfalfa or toasted slivered
almonds, for decoration

Place breasts and stock cubes in a pan with enough water to cover. Bring to the boil then simmer on very low heat for 8 minutes. Remove and when slightly cooled cut into julienne strips. Set aside and chill.

Combine mayonnaise and sour cream. Sprinkle apple with lemon juice and mix with celery and grapes. Fold in chicken strips.

Slice melons. Decorate as desired. Serve with mayonnaise.
Note: Filling can be made up 24 hours ahead, covered with gladwrap and stored in refrigerator until required.

Serves 4–6

SMOKED CHICKEN SURPRISE

1 smoked chicken
½ red cabbage, shredded
2 tablespoons red wine vinegar
or raspberry vinegar
freshly ground pepper
1 teaspoon salt
1 tablespoon caraway seeds
3 tablespoons pine nuts, lightly
toasted

Carve chicken into thin slices, cover and set aside. Unsuitable parts of chicken can be served on another occasion. Sprinkle cabbage with vinegar, pepper and salt. Pour boiling water over to cover and allow to rest for 15 minutes. Drain and sprinkle with caraway seeds. Chill in refrigerator.

When required, fill chicken slices with pickled cabbage and roll up. Spear with toothpicks if necessary. Sprinkle lightly with pine nuts and serve either on individual plates or set out like flower petals on a platter.

Serves 6

Chicken and Rock Melon Salad

ENTERTAINING IDEAS

You're having a party — a barbecue, a gathering on the terrace or a buffet on the back verandah. Suddenly you need some of those reliable favourites like potato salad, rice salad, tabouli and coleslaw. We've included all these recipes and many others to fit in with party fare. Why not add some unusual salads such as Rickshaw Salad, Mexican Meat Ball Salad or Spicy Oriental Seafood Salad? They're prepared in a jiffy and guaranteed to impress any party guest.

BLUE CHEESE COLESLAW

Using a blue cheese such as blue vein or Stilton, refrigerate the cheese before attempting to crumble it. The cheese will then break into fine crumbs and blend beautifully with the other coleslaw ingredients.

3 Granny Smith apples, cored and chopped
3–5 cups thinly shredded cabbage
125 g blue cheese, crumbled
1 cup sour cream
3 tablespoons grated Cheddar cheese
2 tablespoons finely chopped shallot
1½ tablespoons fresh lemon juice
1 tablespoon snipped chives
1 tablespoon red wine vinegar
½ teaspoon salt
½ teaspoon freshly ground pepper

Combine all ingredients in a large salad bowl. Toss well until the cabbage and apple are thoroughly coated with sauce. Cover and chill before serving.

Serves 4–6

PICKLED COLESLAW

Mixing a hot dressing through the coleslaw imparts a special, tangy flavour. Prepare well in advance and refrigerate before serving at your next barbecue.

1 cup salad oil
¾ cup sugar
¾ cup cider vinegar
1 large head cabbage, shredded
2 medium-sized carrots, coarsely grated
1 onion, finely sliced
1 green capsicum, seeded and finely sliced
1 tablespoon French mustard powder
1 teaspoon celery seeds
salt

Combine oil, sugar and vinegar in a saucepan and bring to the boil over medium-high heat.

Combine cabbage, carrots, onion and capsicum in a large heat-proof bowl. Sprinkle with mustard powder, celery seeds and salt, and toss to blend well.

Pour hot oil mixture over vegetables and mix well. Cover and chill for 24 hours. Drain coleslaw well before serving.

Serves 12

COLESLAW

1 medium-sized carrot
1 Granny Smith apple, cored
500 g cabbage, finely shredded
2 tablespoons mayonnaise (see recipe)
2 tablespoons yoghurt
2 tablespoons lemon juice
salt and freshly ground black pepper

Grate carrot and apple finely and combine with cabbage. Mix mayonnaise and yoghurt until smooth, stir in lemon juice, salt and pepper, then stir into the coleslaw, mixing thoroughly. Serve with frankfurts, cold ham or hard-boiled eggs.

Serves 4

POTATO SALAD

2 litres chicken stock
1 kg pontiac potatoes, peeled
¼ cup fresh mint sprigs

Dressing
1 cup mayonnaise (see recipe)
½ cup sour cream
freshly ground black pepper
½ teaspoon mustard powder

Bring stock to the boil in a large saucepan. Add potatoes and mint and cook for 15 minutes or until just tender. Drain and cool the potatoes then cut into 1.5 cm cubes.

Combine the dressing ingredients. Place potatoes in a salad bowl and fold through the dressing. Cover and refrigerate before serving.

Variations
The following ingredients may be added to create colourful and flavoursome variations.
2 bacon rashers, cooked crisply, then crumbled
1 cup green peas or corn kernels, cooked and drained
1 tablespoon French grain mustard

Serves 4–6

DILL-MUSTARD POTATO SALAD

2 litres chicken stock
1 kg new baby potatoes,
unpeeled
¾ cup vegetable oil
1 egg, room temperature
3 tablespoons Dijon-style
mustard
2 tablespoons finely chopped
fresh dill or 2 teaspoons dried
1 teaspoon red wine vinegar
1 teaspoon lemon juice
freshly ground black pepper
½ cup sour cream
3 celery stalks, thinly sliced
1 onion, thinly sliced
½ bunch chives, snipped

Combine stock and potatoes and bring to boil over high heat. Reduce heat and cook potatoes just until tender. Drain immediately and rinse with cold water to cool. Drain potatoes well.

In a food processor or blender combine 3 tablespoons oil, egg, mustard, dill, vinegar, lemon juice and pepper and blend until mixture is slightly thickened, about 10 seconds. With machine running, slowly pour remaining oil through feed tube in thin, steady stream and mix well. Add sour cream and blend 3 seconds to combine.

Slice potatoes into quarters and combine in a salad bowl with celery and onion. Pour over the dressing and fold through the salad. Cover and refrigerate until ready to serve. Garnish with chives.

Serves 6

POTATO SALAD WITH PESTO MAYONNAISE

1.5 kg small new potatoes
salt
2 cups pesto mayonnaise (see
recipe)
¼ cup pine nuts
fresh basil leaves

Wash and scrub new potatoes if necessary. Cook in boiling, salted water until just tender, about 20 minutes depending on their size. Drain and cool.

Make pesto mayonnaise. Fold through just warm potatoes and spoon into a serving bowl. Lightly toast pine nuts in a dry frying pan and sprinkle over the potato salad. Decorate with fresh basil leaves.

Serves 4–6

Dill-Mustard Potato Salad

Arzberg plate

Rice Salad

RICE SALAD

1½ cups long-grain rice
salt
¼ cup vinaigrette (see recipe)
½ telegraph cucumber
½ red capsicum, seeded and
chopped
½ bunch shallots, sliced
4–5 fresh hot chillies, finely
chopped
½ cup chopped fresh parsley
½ cup mayonnaise (see recipe)

Cook long-grain rice in a large pan of boiling salted water for 15 minutes or until just tender. Drain. While still warm toss through vinaigrette. Peel cucumber, leaving a little of the green on, scoop out seeds and chop finely.

Toss salad vegetables through rice with most of the chopped parsley, reserving some for decoration. Fold through mayonnaise. Serve sprinkled with reserved chopped parsley.

Serves 6

CURRIED RICE SALAD

60 g butter
1½ cups long-grain rice
2 teaspoons mustard seeds
few cardamom pods
2 cm piece cinnamon stick
¼ teaspoon turmeric
pinch powdered saffron
salt
½ cup raisins
2 stalks celery, chopped
½ red apple, finely chopped
¾ cup curried mayonnaise (see
recipe)

Melt butter in a heavy-based saucepan. Add rice, mustard seeds, cardamom pods, cinnamon stick and turmeric. Toss over a gentle heat for 1 minute. Add water to the pan to cover the rice with 2 cm water. Add saffron and salt. Bring to the boil and cook uncovered for 1 minute. Cover, lower heat to very low and cook 10 minutes. Remove lid and turn rice out into large bowl.

Remove cinnamon stick and cardamom pods. Separate rice with a fork and fold through remaining ingredients when cool.

Serves 6

CRUNCHY SWEET POTATO SALAD

Sweet potatoes make a refreshing addition to a salad.

2 cups peeled and grated
uncooked sweet potato
1¼ cups finely chopped green
capsicum
1 cup finely chopped almonds or
cashews
½ cup diced peeled cucumber
3 tablespoons unflavoured
yoghurt
lettuce leaves, washed and dried
cucumber slices, to garnish

Combine sweet potato, capsicum, nuts and ½ cup cucumber in large bowl and toss lightly. Add yoghurt and gently fold through the salad.

Arrange lettuce leaves on a platter. Mound salad in centre and garnish with cucumber slices.

Serves 6

RICE NECTAR

1½ cups rice (white or brown)
6 cups water (more if using
brown rice)
6 chicken stock cubes
5 tablespoons walnut or olive oil
2 tablespoons lemon juice
1 tablespoon tarragon vinegar
1 bunch chives, snipped
salt and freshly ground pepper
4 mandarins or 2 oranges, peeled
and sliced
12 shallots, thinly sliced
8 radishes, thinly sliced
3 tablespoons pine nuts or
cashew nuts

Cook rice in water with stock cubes until tender. Drain and place in a bowl. Mix the next 4 ingredients in a glass jar, shake well and pour over drained rice while still warm. Season to taste, cover and refrigerate until required.

To serve, fold in remaining ingredients. For a more substantial salad, serve with left-over poultry or meat. Either dice meat and fold through, or serve separately.

Serves 6

57

MACARONI AND ZUCCHINI SALAD (WITH CRUNCHY PEANUT DRESSING)

250 g zucchini, sliced
salt
1 cup sliced mushrooms
1 cup cooked wholemeal macaroni
¾ cup light cream
¼ cup crunchy peanut butter
½ cup mayonnaise
1 tablespoon honey
1 tablespoon white vinegar
2 tablespoons lemon juice
½ cup roasted peanuts, to garnish

Place zucchini on kitchen paper, sprinkle with salt and allow to stand for 30 minutes. Rinse under cold water and pat dry. Combine zucchini, mushrooms and macaroni in salad bowl. Chill while preparing dressing.

Place all remaining ingredients except peanuts, in blender and whip until smooth but not too thick. Coat salad lightly with dressing.

Chill well and serve garnished with toasted peanuts. Extra dressing will keep well in refrigerator.

Serves 6

PASTA SALAD

250 g spiralli pasta
4 yellow or green zucchini, sliced
½ bunch green onions, sliced
1 green capsicum, sliced
1 punnet cherry tomatoes
1 cup mayonnaise (see recipe)
¼ cup chopped fresh herbs

Cook pasta in boiling salted water until tender. Drain and cool. Blanch zucchini in boiling salted water for 30 seconds. Refresh under cold running water and drain well. Place all salad ingredients together in a bowl and spoon over mayonnaise. Fold through to incorporate. Sprinkle with chopped fresh herbs to serve.

Serves 6

MACARONI MELANGE

500 g macaroni elbow pieces
1 tablespoon oil
4 tablespoons vinaigrette dressing (see recipe)
1 capsicum, seeded and diced
4 dill pickles, thickly sliced
6–8 radishes, sliced
6–8 shallots, chopped
¼ kg strong Cheddar, diced
8 slices salami, cut into strips
black olives

Cook macaroni pieces *al dente*, adding oil to boiling water to prevent adhesion. Drain well and while still warm cover with dressing. Add remaining ingredients, toss well and serve immediately.

Serves 4–6

RICKSHAW SALAD

125 g snow peas, topped and tailed
½ Chinese cabbage, shredded
250 g bean sprouts, washed and dried
4 tablespoons mung beans
440 g can whole baby corn spears, drained
125 g button mushrooms, thinly sliced
6–8 shallots, julienned retaining most of green
½ red capsicum, julienned

Dressing
5 tablespoons olive oil
1 tablespoon white wine vinegar
juice 1 lemon
1 tablespoon soy sauce
2 tablespoons almond slivers and 2 tablespoons sesame seeds, toasted to garnish

Steam snow peas for 3 minutes and when cool, combine with all salad vegetables. Combine dressing ingredients in a screw-top jar and shake well. Pour over vegetable mix and allow to mature at least 30 minutes before serving. Top with toasted almond slivers and sesame seeds and serve with skewered meat or fresh prawns.

Serves 8–10

GADO GADO

This Indonesian vegetable salad makes an interesting starter or main meal salad.

200 g green beans, chopped
½ Chinese cabbage, shredded
1 cucumber, peeled and cut in matchsticks
2 carrots, peeled and sliced diagonally
1 cup bean sprouts
3 hard-boiled eggs, peeled and quartered

Peanut Dressing
1 cup raw peanuts
½ cup peanut oil
1 large onion, finely chopped
2 cloves garlic, crushed
1 teaspoon chilli powder
½ teaspoon prawn paste
1½ cups coconut cream
pinch raw sugar
grated rind and juice 1 lime

Blanch beans in boiling salted water for a few minutes. Refresh under cold water and drain well. Arrange salad vegetables on a large flat platter with egg quarters.

For the peanut dressing, roast peanuts at 190°C (372°F) for 10 minutes until golden brown. Remove and rub the skins off using a clean tea towel. Cool and grind into a paste in a food processor.

Heat oil in a wok and fry onion, garlic, chilli powder and prawn paste for a few minutes. Add peanut paste and coconut cream. Bring to the boil and stir in sugar, grated lime rind and juice. Add salt if desired. Serve dressing at room temperature, either spooned over vegetable salad or separately.

Serves 6

Top: Gado Gado
Bottom: Rickshaw Salad

GINGERED CALAMARI SALAD

Dressing
2 cloves garlic, minced
1 cm piece ginger root, chopped
4 tablespoons oil
1 tablespoon soy sauce
juice ½ lemon
2 tablespoons dry sherry

Salad
500 g calamari, cut in rings
juice 1 lemon
2 tablespoons oil
freshly ground pepper
1 red capsicum, seeded and cut in rings
1 green capsicum, seeded and cut in rings
1 leek, white part only, shredded
4 tablespoons shredded bamboo shoots, finely chopped

Combine dressing ingredients in food processor or a screw-top jar. Set aside for at least ½ an hour to mature. Pour boiling water over calamari and simmer for no more than 4 minutes. If overcooked calamari becomes rubbery. Drain and sprinkle with lemon juice, oil and pepper. Allow to cool and prepare remaining vegetables. To serve, cover calamari with prepared dressing, folding in vegetables last of all.

Serves 6

SPICY ORIENTAL SEAFOOD SALAD

500 g scallops
500 g cooked prawns, peeled
125 g snow peas, topped and tailed
3 stalks celery, finely chopped
1 red capsicum, julienned
6 shallots
440 g can sliced water chestnuts
450 g can whole baby corn

Piquant Dressing
1 clove garlic, crushed
3 tablespoons oil
2 tablespoons white wine vinegar
2 tablespoons dry sherry
2 tablespoons sesame oil
2 tablespoons dry mustard
3 tablespoons soy sauce

Poach scallops in water to cover for 1–2 minutes only. Remove with slotted spoon and set aside to cool with prawns. Steam snow peas for 3 minutes and plunge into iced water to refresh and crisp. Blanch celery in boiling water for 1 minute, plunge into iced water and drain.

Mix all ingredients in a bowl and toss with prepared dressing. To make dressing combine all ingredients in a screw-top jar. This salad is nice served with cold rice cooked in coconut milk or, if you feel extravagant, wild rice. It can also be served with a rice nectar salad (see recipe).

Serves 6–8

TAHITIAN FISH SALAD

In this recipe the lemon juice turns the fish white and it will look cooked. Avoid using a metal spoon or utensils when preparing Tahitian fish salad.

1.5 kg firm white fish fillets
juice 3 lemons
2 medium-sized onions, very finely sliced
2 cups coconut milk
lettuce leaves, washed
salt and freshly ground pepper

Remove all skin from fish fillets. Check for bones and remove, if any. Dice fish and place in a bowl, covering with lemon juice. Chill for at least 30 minutes until fish is white and will flake like cooked fish.

Drain fish in a colander or sieve, pressing gently with back of a wooden spoon to squeeze out any remaining liquid. Put fish mixture in a bowl, add onion and enough coconut milk to coat the fish. Toss gently to coat well.

Serve fish salad on lettuce leaves arranged either in individual dishes or a large salad bowl.

Serves 4–6

MARINARA SALAD

Warm Dressing
2 cloves garlic, crushed
1 teaspoon salt
½ cup chopped parsley
1 cup chopped fresh dill
2 tablespoons grated Parmesan
cheese
½ cup stock (made with 2
chicken cubes)
½ cup oil
juice 1 lemon and grated rind ½
lemon

Salad
2 tablespoons oil
1 bunch shallots, peeled and
thinly sliced
2 cloves garlic, finely chopped
2 cups fish stock
½ kg scallops
½ kg uncooked peeled prawns
(heads removed for fish stock)
2 large carrots, julienned
1 litre water
juice 1 lemon
1 teaspoon salt
½ cup chopped fresh dill
freshly ground pepper
1 packet Conchiglie rigate (shell-
shaped pasta)

Combine dressing ingredients, mix well and set aside in a small saucepan. To make salad, heat oil and saute shallots and garlic until softened. Add fish stock made from discarded prawn heads. Reduce heat, add scallops and poach for 1–2 minutes only. Remove with slotted spoon and keep warm. Add prawns to stock and remove as soon as they turn opaque. Add to reserved scallops. Do not overcook as both will shrink and lose their taste. Increase heat to reduce stock to approximately half quantity. Add all remaining ingredients.

To assemble, cook shell-shaped pasta *al dente* and drain well. Heat dressing, pour over pasta and mix well. Serve pasta topped with seafood mixture at room temperature.

Serves 8

Left to right: Gingered Calamari Salad, Spicy Oriental Seafood Salad, Marinara Salad

Sasaki Wings plates

ROLLED SMOKED TROUT WITH PALM HEARTS AND MUSHROOM CAPS

2 smoked trout, filleted
125 g soft Philadelphia cream cheese
100 g horseradish relish
1 teaspoon salt
425 g can hearts of palm
2 mushroom caps per serving, stems removed
2 tablespoons wine vinegar
1 punnet watercress

Place trout fillets carefully on a plate. Blend cheese with horseradish and salt until smooth. Using a spatula first dipped in hot water, spread this mixture lightly over each fillet. Halve each of the hearts of palm and place on top of fillets. Roll up and, if necessary, spear with a toothpick. Cover and chill until required.

Flute mushroom caps with a knife as if making a flower. Place in a saucepan with vinegar and enough water to cover. Bring to the boil and simmer 2 minutes. Remove with a slotted spoon and allow to cool. When ready to serve, place 2 fillets per person on individual plates, add 2 mushroom caps and decorate with trimmed watercress.

Serves 2

SMOKED SALMON AMBROSIA

4 large ripe peaches
1 ripe avocado
2 tablespoons soft Philadelphia cream cheese
juice 1 lime or lemon
¼ teaspoon salt
1 tablespoon fresh pink peppercorns
12 slices smoked salmon

Pour boiling water over peaches, prick skin and peel. Allow to cool. When cool, halve and take out stones.

Mix the next 4 ingredients until smooth. Fill peach halves and decorate with a few pink peppercorns. Serve 2 peach halves per person with smoked salmon slices on toast triangles.

Serves 4

PRAWN AND CHEESE SALAD WITH MELON

500 g medium-sized cooked prawns, shelled and deveined
125 g Edam cheese, diced
60 g snow peas, blanched
1 small rock melon, seeded
¾ cup mayonnaise (see recipe)
1 teaspoon curry powder
¼ cup light sour cream
salt and freshly ground pepper
fresh dill sprigs, to garnish

Combine prawns, cheese and snow peas in a serving bowl. Cut the melon into pieces, or balls if you have a melon baller and add to bowl. Mix mayonnaise, curry powder and sour cream together and fold through salad. Taste and adjust seasoning. Garnish with dill, cover and chill until serving time.

Serves 4–6

SMOKED SALMON AND DILL FARFALLE

200 g smoked salmon
250 g Philadelphia light cream cheese
2 tablespoons cream
2 tablespoons sour cream
250 g farfalle (bow-shaped pasta)
2 tablespoons finely chopped fresh dill
2 tablespoons finely chopped chives
½ teaspoon salt

Slice salmon into strips and set aside. Blend cheese with both creams until smooth but not liquid.

Cook pasta for 12 minutes, adding a little oil to the boiling water to prevent sticking; stir occasionally. Drain in colander and rinse under hot water. Drain again. Place in warmed bowl and immediately stir in cheese mixture, dill and chives.

Season to taste and fold in half the salmon pieces. Serve on individual plates topped with slivers of remaining salmon to decorate. Best served tepid but can also be eaten cold. This dish is an excellent starter for 6 but will also serve as a light luncheon dish for 4.

Serves 4–6

SALADE NICOISE

This famous salad from Nice is a meal in itself when served with French bread. It also makes a good accompaniment to a meal, such as fish stew, that needs a vegetable and a salad. Leave out the tuna when the salad is to go with fish or meat dishes. There are as many ways to make this salad as there are cooks in Nice!

1 bunch curly endive
1 cos lettuce
3 tomatoes, sliced
150 g French beans, blanched
200 g pontiac or new potatoes, cooked and diced
3 hard-boiled eggs, sliced
1 onion, thinly sliced
1 green capsicum, thinly sliced
12 black olives
425 g can tuna, drained and flaked
½ cup finely chopped fresh parsley or chervil

Dressing
1 clove garlic
4 anchovy fillets, drained
freshly ground black pepper
pinch sugar
1 teaspoon finely chopped fresh basil or ½ teaspoon dried basil
2 tablespoons white wine vinegar
4 tablespoons olive oil

Line a large salad bowl with endive and lettuce. Arrange all the other ingredients attractively on the lettuce. Prepare the dressing by pounding garlic in a mortar and pestle. Add the anchovies, pepper, sugar and basil and continue to pound. Combine this mixture with vinegar and olive oil. Pour over the salad and serve.

Serves 4–6

Top: Salade Nicoise
Bottom: Prawn and Cheese Salad with Melon

SPINACH, AVOCADO AND BACON SALAD

If you have spinach or silverbeet growing in your garden, use the young, small leaves in this salad. It is much cheaper than lettuce and the bacon makes a delicious dressing.

250 g spinach
4 bacon rashers, rind removed and chopped
1 teaspoon olive oil
1 ripe avocado, peeled and sliced

Dressing
3 tablespoons olive oil
1 tablespoon white wine vinegar
pinch sugar
freshly ground black pepper

Trim stalk away from the spinach and wash in cold water. Pat dry with a cloth then refrigerate spinach for 1 hour. Tear leaves into bite-sized pieces. Fry bacon in olive oil until crisp and golden. Remove and combine with spinach and avocado in a salad bowl.

To make the dressing, combine all ingredients together in a screw-top jar and shake until well blended. Just before serving salad, toss through the dressing.

Serves 6

TOMATOES WITH AVOCADO

The perfect accompaniment to poached fish.

6 medium-sized tomatoes, cored and peeled
salt and freshly ground pepper, to taste
1 large ripe avocado, chopped
¼ cup vinaigrette (see recipe)
1 green or red capsicum
1 tablespoon finely chopped shallots
1 tablespoon chopped fresh dill or 1 teaspoon dried dill

Slice off the round end of the tomatoes and scoop out the seeds and membranes. Season shell with salt and pepper, invert and leave to drain on absorbent paper.

Combine avocado with remaining ingredients, cover and chill for 30 minutes. Spoon avocado mixture into tomato shells.

Serves 6

GREEN JADE SALAD

1 bunch watercress
4 stalks celery, finely sliced
4 tablespoons mung beans
1 small punnet alfalfa sprouts
1 ripe avocado, peeled and diced
juice 2 lemons
3 tablespoons tamari or 2 tablespoons soy sauce
2 tablespoons finely chopped fresh basil
2 tablespoons sesame seeds, toasted

Wash and dry watercress, removing thickest stems. Crisp in tea towel placed in refrigerator. When required place in salad bowl and add next 3 ingredients. Sprinkle avocado with lemon juice and tamari and fold through. Season with basil and sesame seeds to serve.

Serves 6

LETTUCE BOWL SALAD

As an elegant addition to your next buffet, serve these intriguing salads which are contained within their own lettuce 'cups'.

Salad
1 iceberg lettuce, separated into leaves
3 tomatoes, sliced
1 endive, separated into leaves
6 bacon rashers
6 quail eggs, hard-boiled and shelled
12 chives, snipped
1 tablespoon pine nuts

Dressing
½ cup mayonnaise (see recipe)
1 teaspoon French mustard
1 teaspoon grated lemon rind
freshly ground black pepper

Wash lettuce and, using a small knife, cut away the stem end of each leaf. Arrange the lettuce 'cups' on a salad platter. Inside each place a few tomato slices and an endive leaf.

Thread bacon onto skewers and grill until crisp. Remove bacon and arrange in salad cups with remaining salad ingredients. Combine all dressing ingredients, mixing until well blended. Spoon a little over the salad just before serving.

Serves 6

CAPSICUM SALAD A LA CREME

3 red capsicums
3 green capsicums
5 tablespoons light sour cream
2 tablespoons chives, chopped
freshly ground pepper
1 bunch watercress, thicker stems removed

Char whole capsicums over a gas burner or place under griller until the skin is almost black; then put in a closed paper bag for 10 minutes to steam. Peel off all charred skin, halve capsicums, remove seeds and slice. Place in a bowl.

Mix sour cream with chives and pepper. Cover capsicum slices with this mixture and fold through gently so as not to break slices. Trim edge of serving bowl with sprigs of watercress and fill the centre with capsicums. This salad is delicious with barbecued meats.

Serves 6–8

BAKED BEETROOT SALAD

4 large beetroot
aluminium foil
1 large Spanish onion
a little oil

Dressing
2 tablespoons raspberry vinegar or red wine vinegar
3 tablespoons olive oil
1 teaspoon caraway seeds (optional)
freshly ground white pepper
salt

Cut stems from beets, wash, dry and wrap each beet in foil, adding ½ teaspoon oil to each packet before sealing. Cut a deep cross into base of onion but do not peel and prepare as for beetroot. Bake at 180°C (350°F) for 1½ hours until tender. (Test with a skewer)

Peel and cut beets into julienne strips, slice onion crosswise and then into halves. Combine in a bowl and cover with remaining ingredients while still warm. Serve tepid or chilled with barbecues or cold meats.

Serves 6

Top: Spinach, Avocado and Bacon Salad
Bottom: Baked Beetroot Salad

SPICY EGG 'N' BACON SALAD

1 butter lettuce, washed and dried
4 rashers bacon, rinds removed and diced
oil for frying
1–2 cloves garlic, chopped
4 slices bread, diced
1 heaped teaspoon sambal oelek or 1 red chilli, seeded and chopped
2 tablespoons black olives
4 hard-boiled eggs, quartered
squeeze lemon juice

Tear lettuce into bite-sized pieces into a bowl. Fry bacon with a little oil and chopped garlic until crisp and golden, tossing continuously. Remove with slotted spoon and keep warm on kitchen paper in low oven. Fry bread croutons in similar fashion and keep warm with bacon. If using, add sambal oelek to hot fat and stir through, or fry chilli lightly in remaining oil.

To serve, combine all ingredients and arrange decoratively in salad bowl, garnishing with olives and egg quarters. Add a squeeze of lemon juice and serve immediately.

Serves 4

HOT VEGETABLE SALAD WITH FRESH BASIL

1 green capsicum, seeded and sliced
300 g cauliflower, cut into florets
200 g beans, strung
300 g cherry tomatoes
60 g butter, melted
salt and freshly ground black pepper
10 fresh basil leaves, finely chopped
1 teaspoon French mustard
sprigs fresh basil to garnish

Blanch capsicum, cauliflower and beans in boiling water for 3 minutes. Drain well then place in a heat-proof dish. Scatter over the tomatoes.

Combine butter, salt, pepper, basil and mustard. Drizzle this dressing over the vegetables and bake at 180°C (350°F) for 10 minutes. Serve at once garnished with extra basil.

Serves 6

Left to right: Spicy Egg 'n' Bacon Salad, Hot Vegetable Salad with Fresh Basil, Mixed Bean Salad, Green Goddess Salad

MIXED BEAN SALAD

An excellent source of fibre, beans can also make a variety of interesting salads. Cooked beans can be stored in the refrigerator for up to 10 days.

½ cup red kidney beans
½ cup black-eyed beans
½ cup chick peas
½ cup butter beans

Dressing
¼ cup olive oil
2 tablespoons lemon juice
1 clove garlic, crushed
3 shallots, chopped
pinch dry mustard
fresh parsley, finely chopped

Soak all beans overnight in water then drain well. Bring to the boil very slowly in fresh water for about 30 minutes. Simmer over low heat for 40 minutes, until tender. Drain beans, rinse and cool.

Put all dressing ingredients, except parsley, in a jar and shake to mix well. Pour over cold beans and mix to coat. Sprinkle with chopped parsley and serve.

Serves 4

GREEN GODDESS SALAD

This famous salad was first created in 1915 at the Palace Hotel in honour of George Arliss, who was then appearing in San Francisco in William Archer's play *The Green Goddess*.

Dressing
8 anchovy fillets, chopped
1 shallot, chopped
2 tablespoons finely chopped
fresh parsley
2 tablespoons finely chopped
fresh tarragon or 1 tablespoon
dried tarragon soaked in vinegar
then drained
2 tablespoons finely chopped
chives
1 cup mayonnaise (see recipe)
¼ cup tarragon vinegar

Salad
1 clove garlic, peeled
1 large cos lettuce
500 g cooked seafood (lobster,
prawns, crab meat) or chicken

In a bowl, combine all dressing ingredients, mixing well. Rub a salad bowl with garlic clove and tear lettuce into bite-sized pieces in the bowl. Pour over dressing then toss lightly. Garnish with desired shellfish or chicken and serve in bowl or on individual salad plates.

Serves 6

Sasaki plates

BROAD BEAN AND PASTA SALAD WITH ORANGE DRESSING

175 g wholemeal macaroni, cooked
2 cups chick peas, cooked
1 cup broad beans, cooked

Orange Dressing
3 tablespoons olive oil
juice 1 orange
1 teaspoon freshly ground black pepper
1 tablespoon finely chopped fresh parsley or chives

Mix pasta, peas and beans together in salad bowl. Shake dressing ingredients together in a jar, pour over salad and toss.

Serves 4

ROSY ROAST BEEF SALAD

4 large potatoes, peeled, boiled and thickly sliced
5 tablespoons mayonnaise (see recipe)
2 tablespoons cream
1 tablespoon horseradish
3 tablespoons tomato sauce
10 shallots, thinly sliced
4 slices roast beef, cut in strips
1-2 tablespoons capers
1 bunch asparagus, blanched or 440 g can asparagus

Cook potatoes and place in a bowl. Mix next 4 ingredients in a jar and shake well before pouring over still warm potatoes.

Sprinkle with shallots and allow to steep for at least 2 hours in a covered bowl placed in refrigerator.

Just before serving add meat and capers and serve with asparagus.

Serves 4-6

VITELLO CRUDO (ITALIAN VEAL SLICES)

6-12 slices of veal schnitzels (cut from leg)
½ cup olive oil
¼ cup lemon juice
3 cloves garlic, crushed with 1 teaspoon salt
4 spurts Tabasco sauce
freshly ground pepper
250 g button mushrooms, thinly sliced

Place veal between 2 sheets of plastic wrap and pound until very thin. Place them on a platter. Beat oil with lemon juice, salted garlic and Tabasco. Pour over meat. Sprinkle liberally with freshly ground pepper. Top with mushroom slices and refrigerate for at least 2 hours. Serve with the salad of your choice.

Serves 6

MINTED LAMB SALAD

500 g cold, cooked lamb fillets, sliced into medallions
½ cup walnuts, chopped
1 tablespoon chopped chives
1 tablespoon chopped fresh mint
125 g cherry tomatoes, halved
1 cucumber, peeled, seeded and diced
juice ½ lemon
3 cups tabouli (see recipe)
fresh sprigs mint, to garnish

Combine all salad ingredients and spoon into a salad bowl. Cover and refrigerate for several hours. Serve well chilled, garnished with mint.

Serves 4-6

MEXICAN MEAT BALL SALAD

500 g topside mince
250 g sausage mince
freshly ground black pepper
1 small onion, finely chopped
1 egg
½ cup flour
oil, for shallow-frying
440 g can baby corn, drained
1 red capsicum, seeded and finely sliced
200 g packet corn chips
small bunch curly endive, torn into leaves

Dressing
1 large tomato, peeled
½ cup mayonnaise (see recipe)
1 tablespoon tomato paste
½ teaspoon Worcestershire sauce
dash Tabasco sauce

Combine first 5 ingredients in a bowl and mix until evenly combined. Using lightly floured hands, roll mixture into 2.5 cm balls.

Heat oil for shallow-frying in a pan. Cook meat balls, a few at a time, turning frequently. Drain on absorbent kitchen paper and allow to cool.

Combine meat balls with remaining salad ingredients and arrange in a salad bowl just before serving.

Place all dressing ingredients in a small bowl and whisk until smooth. Spoon over salad and serve.

Serves 6-8

Top: Vitello Crudo
Bottom: Rosy Roast Beef Salad

SPICED RED CABBAGE WITH LAMB NOISETTES

3 thick lamb noisettes
½ head red cabbage, shredded
5 tablespoons vinaigrette
dressing (see recipe)
1 tablespoon caraway seeds
1 tablespoon chopped fresh
rosemary
2 tablespoons pine nuts, lightly
toasted

Pan-fry lamb lightly on both sides in minimum amount of oil then place in a pre-heated moderate oven 180°C (350°F) for 20 minutes. Remove and allow to cool. When required remove skewers or threads from lamb, and slice. Place shredded cabbage in a salad bowl. Warm vinaigrette, pour over cabbage and blend. Toss through caraway seeds and rosemary. Place tossed cabbage on a serving platter and top with overlapping slices of lamb. Sprinkle with pine nuts.

Serves 6

CHICKEN AND FRUIT SALAD

1.5 kg cold chicken
50 g noodles, cooked
1 orange, peeled and segmented
4 slices pineapple, cut in pieces
200 g apple, sliced
3 tablespoons lemon juice
190 g mandarin, peeled and
segmented
½ cup sour cream
3 tablespoons mayonnaise (see
recipe)
2 tablespoons mango chutney
1 tablespoon tomato sauce
salt and freshly ground pepper

Skin and dice chicken (no bones). Combine with all other ingredients in a serving bowl. Mix well and refrigerate.

Serves 6

GOURMET DUCK AND ALMOND SALAD

1.4 kg duck (minimum)
1 onion
½ lemon
½ orange
1 clove garlic, chopped
small piece ginger root
salt and freshly ground pepper
butter
juice 1 orange
1 bunch watercress
1 mignonette lettuce
2 tablespoons almond slivers,
toasted

Fruit Marinade
1 tablespoon chopped ginger root
1 clove garlic, crushed
4 tablespoons oil
1 tablespoon raspberry vinegar
or red wine
2 tablespoons honey
1 tablespoon soy sauce
1 tablespoon red wine
¼ teaspoon cinnamon
12 apricots, fresh or dried

Stuff duck with onion, lemon, orange and garlic. Rub outer skin with ginger root, sprinkle with seasoning. Place in baking dish with 2.5 cm water. Rub breast with butter and cover with foil. Bake at 180°C (350°F) for 1 hour.

Remove foil, baste, pour orange juice over and cook a further hour basting occasionally. When cooked, cool and slice duck, discarding bones. Cover and refrigerate until required.

To prepare the marinade, saute ginger and garlic in oil over medium heat 1 minute. Remove from heat, and stir in next 5 items. Return to heat to warm through only, then immediately pour over apricots in an ovenproof dish. Allow to marinate overnight or for at least 2 hours.

To serve, line a salad bowl with trimmed watercress and torn bite-sized lettuce. Fill dish with duck slices, top with apricots and drizzle with marinade. Sprinkle with toasted almond slivers.

Serves 6–8

PIQUANT ANCHOVY SALAD

1 cos lettuce
6 slices bread, diced in croutons
oil, for frying
freshly ground pepper
1 small tin anchovies, roughly
chopped
12 pimiento stuffed olives
6 shallots, finely chopped
12 capers
1 egg, lightly boiled (1 minute)
2 tablespoons freshly grated
Parmesan cheese

Dressing
1 tablespoon Worcestershire
sauce
2 tablespoons wine vinegar
1 teaspoon horseradish
juice ½ lemon
dash Tabasco sauce

Rinse lettuce, tear into bite-sized pieces and allow to dry and crisp, wrapped in a tea towel in the refrigerator. Prepare dressing by combining ingredients in a screw-top jar and shaking well. Set aside.

Fry bread croutons in oil, tossing continually to prevent burning. Remove with slotted spoon and sprinkle with freshly ground pepper.

Coat lettuce pieces with dressing and toss well. Add anchovies, olives, shallots and capers and toss again. Break egg into salad and mix well. Top with croutons and dust lightly with cheese.
Note: For a picnic, all ingredients can be taken separately and assembled on site.

Serves 6–8

Spiced Red Cabbage with Lamb Noisettes

POOR MAN'S CAVIAR

salt
5 eggplants
a little oil
4 tablespoons chopped fresh parsley
5 tablespoons white wine vinegar
2 tablespoons lemon juice
2 tablespoons chopped fresh mint
2 teaspoons salt
4 cloves garlic, finely minced
1 teaspoon freshly ground pepper
½ teaspoon cinnamon
½ teaspoon dried coriander

Preheat oven on 180°C (350°F). Grease baking sheet and sprinkle with salt. Halve eggplants lengthways and set, cut side down, on baking sheet. Bake until tender, about 45 minutes. Remove from oven and cool slightly, then peel and chop finely. Drain in a colander.

Combine with all remaining ingredients using a food processor, cover and chill for at least 24 hours. To serve, place in 2 or 3 separate bowls surrounded by either toast squares or suitable biscuits for dipping.

Serves 25

MUSHROOM SALAD

450 g button mushrooms
6 tablespoons olive oil
2 tablespoons fresh lemon juice
salt and freshly ground pepper
½ teaspoon Dijon-style mustard (optional)
150 mL carton sour cream or equal parts whipped double cream mixed with unflavoured yoghurt

Wash and wipe mushrooms, remove stalks and slice caps very thinly. Combine oil, lemon juice, salt, pepper and mustard and blend well.

Serve sliced mushrooms in a large bowl, cream in a small one and vinaigrette in another.

Serves 4

GOLDEN ORB SALAD

1 butter lettuce
2 tablespoons walnut oil
juice ½ lemon
2 oranges, peeled and thinly sliced
2 tablespoons finely chopped fresh chives
2 tablespoons finely chopped fresh basil
freshly ground white pepper
2 tablespoons pecan nuts

Retaining outer leaves of lettuce, cut out centre leaves and set aside. Rinse outer leaves carefully, trim stem and shake dry. Use to line a glass salad bowl.

Tear heart of lettuce into bite-sized pieces in a separate bowl. Coat these well with oil then sprinkle with lemon juice and toss.

Halve orange slices and fold through. Add chives and basil and mix in well. Turn mixture into lined salad bowl and top with nuts to serve. This salad is delicious with poached duck fillets or other cold poultry.

Serves 6

BLENDER GUACAMOLE

2 large tomatoes, peeled
1 large onion, roughly chopped
3 cloves garlic
1 chilli, seeded
1 teaspoon salt
2 teaspoons Madras curry powder
juice 2 limes
3 ripe avocados
1 tablespoon chopped fresh coriander leaves

Combine first 7 ingredients in food processor and blend well. Peel avocados and add to mixture. Place in a bowl, cover with plastic wrap and refrigerate until required. It will keep well for 24 hours. Sprinkle with coriander and serve with corn chips.

Serves 12

TABOULI

This delightful Middle Eastern salad has become very popular in recent years. Not only is it very healthy, it tastes wonderfully refreshing made with plenty of chopped parsley, and mint, combined with lemon juice and the nutty flavour of the cracked wheat (burghul). Serve Tabouli with flat pita bread, hummus and black olives as part of a traditional mezze (hors d'oeuvre), or as an accompaniment to grilled or barbecued meats.

¾ cup burghul (cracked wheat)
1½ cups chopped fresh parsley
⅔ cup chopped fresh mint
1 large tomato, chopped
½ bunch shallots, chopped
salt and freshly ground black pepper
juice 1 lemon
3 tablespoons olive oil

Soak the burghul in water to cover for 5 minutes. Drain well. Place in a bowl with remaining ingredients and toss well to thoroughly mix. Serve the same day.

Serves 4

BEETROOT SALAD

1 kg baby beetroot
½ bunch watercress
1 cup horseradish sour cream dressing (see recipe)
½ bunch chives, snipped

Steam or simmer beetroots in their jackets until tender, about 40 minutes depending on their size. Cool in a bowl of cold water and slip their skins off.

Halve or quarter and arrange in a salad bowl with watercress. Fold through dressing or serve separately. Decorate with snipped chives.

Serves 4

Top: Golden Orb Salad
Bottom: Mushroom Salad

73

CHEESE PLATTER

This cheese platter is suitable for summer or winter when, although our selection of fresh fruit is good, it is still limited. Either pear or apple wedges can be offered. This selection of cheeses would be nice served with port or liqueurs and after-dinner coffee.

nasturtium leaves, well washed and dried
300 g blue vein cheese
300 g Edam cheese
300 g Swiss cheese
300 g Cheshire cheese or matured Cheddar cheese
nasturtium flowers, washed and shaken dry
50 g unblanched almonds
100 g pecans or Brazil nuts
60 g good quality dried apricots
60 g dried muscatels or raisins
2 pears, peeled
little lemon juice
crackers to serve

Place nasturtium leaves on a serving platter. Arrange cheeses on the leaves, leaving the centre free. Decorate platter with flowers. Combine nuts and dried fruits and place in the centre of the platter.

Halve pears lenthways. Cut into wedges, removing the centre core. Brush lightly with lemon juice. Arrange pears on the platter. Serve crackers separately.

Serves 6–8

CHEESE AND FRESH FRUIT PLATTER

250 g fresh ricotta cheese
fresh grape leaves, well washed
300 g feta cheese
300–500 g Camembert cheese
300 g semi-matured Cheddar cheese
50 g purple or green grapes
1 small rock melon, peeled, seeded and sliced
3 kiwifruit, peeled and cut in wedges
selection of crackers, to serve

Place ricotta cheese in a sieve and drain for 5 minutes. Arrange grape leaves on a serving platter. Carefully put ricotta cheese on grape leaves, moulding into a neat shape. Arrange other cheeses on the platter.

Wash grapes and separate into small bunches. Attractively arrange fruit on platter and cover until serving time. Serve crackers separately.

Serves 6–8

CHEESE AND PICKLES PLATTER

300 g vintage Cheddar cheese
250 g Pecorino cheese
250 g Haloumy cheese
250 g Pastorello cheese
250 g smoked cheese
8–10 dill cucumbers
45 g black olives
1 red capsicum, seeded and sliced
½ bunch shallots, trimmed and chilled
water biscuits, to serve

Arrange cheeses attractively on a serving platter. In the centre of platter, arrange dill cucumbers, olives and capsicum. Serve shallots and water biscuits separately.

Serves 6–8

PURELY PORTABLE

The salad sandwich has been revolutionised! Whether you use a crusty French stick, white or wholemeal bread as your base, these tempting, appetising fillings will give you a whole new perspective on salad sandwiches. New combinations like Blue Cheese and Dates or Anchovy, Walnut and Celery make the most delicious sandwiches you've ever tasted. There are inventive ideas for the picnic basket too. The Picnic Tomato Platter and the Lebanese Cheese Roll will satisfy any fresh air appetite. You need never rely on Vegemite again.

PATE AND BRIE ON RYE

250 g pate de foie gras or another good liver pate
4 slices rye bread, toasted
125 g Brie, cut into triangles
watercress leaves
½ red capsicum, sliced

Slice pate thinly and place on toasted rye bread. Arrange Brie triangles on one half of the bread. Put watercress leaves on the other half. Serve garnished with capsicum strips.

Serves 4

PECORINO AND TOMATO ON RYE

4 slices rye bread
8 slices tomato
90 g pecorino cheese, crumbled
2 slices apple

Top rye bread with tomato slices. Divide pecorino cheese between bread slices. Cut apple slices in half. Stand cut edge of apple upright in centre of cheese to garnish.

Serves 4

ANCHOVY, WALNUT AND CELERY PUMPERNICKEL

6 slices pumpernickel bread
3 lettuce leaves, washed and torn
250 g cream cheese
30 g blue cheese eg blue vein, crumbled
2 tablespoons yoghurt
¼ cup chopped walnuts
¼ cup chopped celery
30 g can anchovies, drained
fresh parsley sprigs, to garnish

Top each slice of pumpernickel bread with lettuce. Combine cream and blue cheeses, yoghurt, walnuts and celery. Spoon a portion of cheese mixture onto each slice of pumpernickel. Top with anchovy and garnish with parsley.

Serves 4–6

TARAMASALATA AND SALAD POCKETS

4–6 pita bread pockets
200 g taramasalata (available from delicatessens)
1 cucumber, peeled and sliced
250 g cottage cheese
freshly ground black pepper
1 bunch snipped chives
1 lettuce leaf, washed and shredded
alfalfa sprouts

Heat the pocket bread briefly under a preheated grill or in a hot oven. Cut bread open or cut in half. Spread each pocket with taramasalata and top with cucumber slices.

Combine cottage cheese, black pepper and chives. Spoon cottage cheese mixture evenly between pockets. Fill with lettuce and alfalfa sprouts.

Serves 4–6

VEGETARIAN PITA BREAD

2 pita bread pockets, heated
2 lettuce leaves, shredded
1 spinach leaf, shredded
½ cup bean sprouts
½ cup alfalfa sprouts
¼ cup roughly chopped walnuts
250 g cottage cheese

Split heated pocket bread. Fill equally with lettuce, spinach, bean sprouts, alfalfa and walnuts. Complete with cottage cheese.

Serves 2

LEBANESE CHEESE ROLL

4 pita bread pockets
½ lettuce, washed and shredded
2 shallots, chopped
½ cup finely chopped fresh parsley
¼ cup finely chopped fresh mint
juice 1 lemon
½ cup olive oil
1 tomato, thinly sliced
250 g Feta cheese, crumbled
¼ cup chopped black olives

Preheat oven to 200°C (400°F), wrap bread in aluminium foil and warm in oven for 5 minutes. Combine lettuce, shallots, parsley, mint, lemon juice, olive oil and tomato. Divide salad between bread pockets, placing on top of the bread. Top with Feta cheese and olives.

To serve, place each bread round on a piece of greaseproof paper about 5 cm longer all round than the bread. Roll up the bread and paper, Swiss roll style, tucking in one end as you roll. Twist the remaining paper to seal.

Serves 4

WHOLEMEAL CHEESE BREAD

Makes 2 loaves
25 g compressed yeast
425 mL warm water
750 g wholemeal flour
1 teaspoon salt
2 tablespoons sugar
¼ cup grated Cheddar cheese
1 onion, finely chopped
1 tablespoon soy flour
2 tablespoons sunflower seeds
1 tablespoon linseeds
1 tablespoon oil
1 tablespoon extra grated Cheddar cheese
1 tablespoon grated Parmesan cheese

Dissolve yeast in 1 cup warm water, leave for 10–20 minutes until the yeast is frothy. Sift together flour, salt and sugar. Make a well and add yeast mixture by blending it to a paste with a little of the flour, then mixing in well. Combine with the next 5 ingredients.

Blend together remaining water and oil. Add to flour mixture and mix to a firm dough. Place dough on a lightly floured board and knead for 10 minutes or until the dough is smooth and elastic. Return dough to an oiled bowl. Cover with plastic wrap and allow to double in size. Punch down dough and form into shapes required.

For loaves: Cut the dough in half and shape into a loaf. Alternatively shape 2 dough pieces into a round.

For plaits: Halve the dough. Divide each piece of dough into 3 pieces and roll into strips. Plait the strips together and tuck under the ends.

For rolls: Cut the dough into number of rolls required. Knead lightly and shape into rounds.

Place dough in greased loaf tins or on baking trays and cover with plastic wrap. Allow to rise in a warm place for 10–20 minutes. Preheat oven to 200°C (400°F). Before baking sprinkle loaves with extra Cheddar and Parmesan cheeses.

Bake loaves for 35–40 minutes and rolls for 15–20 minutes. Tap bread to test; if cooked it will sound hollow. Turn out onto wire rack to cool.

Wholemeal Cheese Bread

BLUE CHEESE AND DATES

*1 slice wholemeal cheese bread
(see recipe)
3 slices green apple, cored
60 g blue cheese, crumbled
3 fresh dates, halved and pitted
chopped fresh parsley, to garnish*

Top bread with apple slices, blue cheese
and dates. Garnish with parsley.

Serves 1

SWISS CHEESE AND HAM

*1 slice wholemeal cheese bread
(see recipe)
1 slice prosciutto ham
1 slice Swiss cheese
1 stuffed green olive*

Top bread with ham, Swiss cheese and
olives.

Serves 1

CAMEMBERT AND CUCUMBER

1 slice wholemeal cheese bread
(see recipe)
1 lettuce leaf
4 slices peeled cucumber
60 g Camembert, sliced
radish slices

Top bread with lettuce, cucumber and Camembert slices. Serve garnished with radish.

Serves 1

SMOKED TURKEY AND CHUTNEY

1 slice wholemeal cheese bread
(see recipe)
1–2 slices smoked turkey
2 teaspoons fruit chutney
2 slices tomato
½ cup grated Cheddar cheese
watercress, to garnish

Place smoked turkey on bread. Spread with chutney and top with tomato then cheese. Serve garnished with watercress.

Serves 1

Left to right: Blue Cheese and Dates, Swiss Cheese and Ham, Camembert and Cucumber, Smoked Turkey and Chutney

PAN BAGNIA

These French sandwiches are sold in cafes all along the coast of Provence through to Monte Carlo and on into the Italian Riviera. What nicer lunch than a French stick (baguette) filled with salade nicoise (see recipe), and a glass of wine.

1 long French stick
1 clove garlic
olive oil
2 ripe tomatoes, sliced
3 hard-boiled eggs, peeled and sliced
½ bunch radishes
100 g can anchovies, drained
1 small lettuce, torn in bite-sized pieces
black olives
freshly ground black pepper

Slice French stick through horizontally and remove some of the centre. Rub the inside of the bread with a cut garlic clove and sprinkle with a little olive oil.

Arrange all ingredients over the bottom half of the French stick. Season with pepper. Cover with the top half of the bread. Tie at intervals with string. Wrap in greaseproof paper to transport. Cut into 4 to serve.

Serves 4

EGG SALAD STICKS

2 small French breadsticks
4 tablespoons mayonnaise
(see recipe)
6 eggs
salt and freshly ground black pepper
4 shallots, chopped
1 cup shredded lettuce or alfalfa sprouts
100 g black caviar

Split the French breadsticks lengthways. Remove a little of the centre, and spread with mayonnaise. Scramble eggs, until creamy. Season well with salt and pepper. Add the shallots. Spread the lettuce or alfalfa over the base of each French breadstick and top with scrambled egg and caviar. Cover with bread lids. Wrap in foil and chill until required.

Serves 4

HERO SALAD LOAF

1 crusty round Italian loaf
⅓ cup olive oil
½ head lettuce, shredded
250 g sliced ham
3 tablespoons coarse seed mustard
3 medium-sized tomatoes, sliced
200 g Gruyere, thinly sliced
5 radishes, sliced
1 Spanish onion, thinly sliced
3 tablespoons capers

Slice the loaf horizontally and remove most of the bread centre. Brush inside lightly with oil. Spread the lettuce over the bread base, top with ham and spread with mustard. Arrange the tomato and cheese slices over, sprinkle with radish and onion slices. Scatter over capers. Cover with lid and wrap tightly with foil. Leave for 1 hour. Cut into wedges to serve.

Serves 4–6

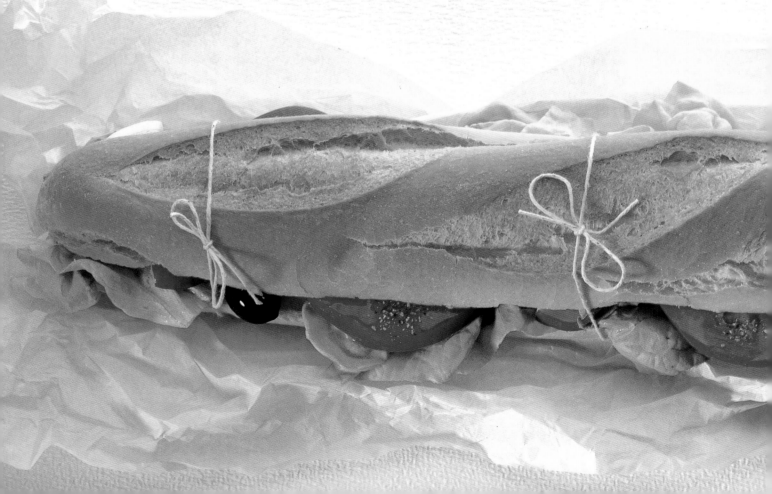

TAPENADE-FILLED FRENCH STICKS

6 hard-boiled eggs
375 g large black olives, pitted
and chopped
3 tablespoons capers, drained
and chopped
185 g can tuna in oil, drained
1 teaspoon Dijon-style mustard
juice ½ lemon
2 tablespoons chopped parsley
1 long slim French stick

Halve eggs and push egg yolks through a coarse sieve. Set aside egg whites (these may be used in another salad). In a bowl combine all salad ingredients. Pound with the end of a rolling pin to form a smooth paste.

Split French stick lengthways and remove bread from the centre. Fill half with the tapenade mixture, mounding it along the length. Top with the remaining half and wrap in aluminium foil. Chill for 1 hour. Cut into 3 cm slices to serve.

Serves 4

WATERCRESS AND SMOKED SALMON LOGS

1 long French breadstick
¾ cup mayonnaise (see recipe)
300 g smoked salmon slices
1 Spanish onion, thinly sliced
freshly ground black pepper
2 cups watercress sprigs
2–3 tablespoons vinaigrette
(see recipe)
¼ cup fresh dill sprigs

Split the French breadstick lengthways. Remove some of the bread centre. Spread halves thickly with the mayonnaise. Lay the smoked salmon over each half, top with onion and season with pepper. Toss the watercress sprigs in vinaigrette. Cover both halves then sprinkle with dill.

Press the halves together and wrap securely with foil. Chill until required. To serve, separate the halves and cut into 10 cm lengths.

Serves 4

SMOKED CHEESE SANDWICH

250 g smoked cheese, grated
1 stalk celery, finely chopped
1 slice ham, chopped
butter
8 slices white bread
4 lettuce leaves
2 tablespoons mayonnaise (see recipe)

Combine smoked cheese, celery and ham. Butter bread and top 4 slices with lettuce and mayonnaise. Add a portion of cheese mixture and top with other slice of bread. Serve cut into quarters.

Serves 4

Pan Bagnia

SPRINGTIME SALAD

1 bunch endive
1 bunch watercress
4 tablespoons vinaigrette made
with Dijon-style mustard (see
recipe)
1 whitloof, sliced in rounds
juice ½ lemon
215 g can beetroot, julienned
12 slices mortadella or devon,
cut in strips
3 hard-boiled eggs, thickly sliced
12 pink or green peppercorns, or
freshly ground pepper

Wash and dry greens, discarding thicker stems of watercress. Tear into bite-sized pieces and coat with vinaigrette dressing. Sprinkle whitloof with lemon juice and add to salad with beetroot and meat strips. To serve, decorate top with sliced hard-boiled eggs and green peppercorns. *Note:* This salad provides a quick and appetising luncheon or travels well to picnics. For the latter, pack all ingredients in separate covered picnic bowls and assemble on site.

Serves 6–8

MEXICAN SALAD TACOS

6–8 taco shells
2 cups finely shredded cabbage
or lettuce
1 cup cooked red beans
100 g chilli cabanossi sausage,
cut into strips
½ red capsicum, chopped
salt and freshly ground black
pepper
¼ teaspoon cumin
3 tablespoons vinaigrette (see
recipe)
1 cup grated Cheddar cheese
½ cup sour cream
paprika

Warm taco shells in the oven at 190°C (375°F) for 5 minutes or until crisp. Remove and cool. Fill each with shredded cabbage. Place the beans in a bowl and add the cabanossi sausage and capsicum. Season with salt, pepper and cumin to taste and toss with the vinaigrette. Use to fill each taco shell. Top with cheese. Serve sour cream separately, sprinkled with a little paprika to garnish.

Serves 6–8

PICNIC TOMATO PLATTER

8–10 large tomatoes
salt and freshly ground pepper
½ cup olive oil
2 onions, finely chopped
¾ cup rice
2 tablespoons currants
2 tablespoons pine nuts
2 tablespoons finely chopped
fresh mint
2 tablespoons finely chopped
fresh parsley

Cut the tops from the tomatoes and using a teaspoon, scoop the centres out reserving the pulp and lids. Sprinkle the insides lightly with salt and turn the tomatoes upside down on absorbent paper to drain.

Heat oil in a pan and saute onions until browned. Stir in tomato pulp, then mix in remaining ingredients. Simmer for 2 minutes, then add 1¼ cups water and cook slowly for 7 minutes or until the rice begins to soften. Season to taste.

Spoon mixture into tomato shells, allowing room at the top for the rice to swell. Replace the tops and brush all over with oil. Arrange on a greased baking tray and cook in an oven preheated to 180°C (350°F) for 35–40 minutes. Serve well chilled.

Serves 4–5

TOMATOES WITH TUNA

6 medium-sized tomatoes, cored
and peeled
200 g can tuna packed in oil
3 eggs, hard-boiled and chopped
1 shallot, chopped
squeeze lemon juice
salt and freshly ground pepper,
to taste
1 tablespoon chopped dill, to
garnish

Cut off the top third of tomatoes and scoop out seeds and membrane. Drain tuna well and flake with a fork. Combine with eggs, shallot and lemon juice. Season to taste. Spoon into the tomato cases and serve garnished with dill.

Serves 6

CASHEW AND BROWN RICE TOMATOES

6 medium-sized tomatoes
30 g butter
4 shallots, chopped
1 cup brown rice, well rinsed
freshly ground black pepper
2 cups chicken stock
60 g cashew nuts
fresh parsley, to garnish

Cut the tops from the tomatoes and using a teaspoon, scoop the centres out reserving the pulp and lids. Sprinkle the insides lightly with salt and turn tomatoes upside down on absorbent paper to drain.

Heat butter in a large pan. Add shallots and rice and cook for 1 minute, stirring constantly. Add pepper and chicken stock, cover pan and bring mixture to the boil. Reduce heat and cook for 20 minutes or until liquid has evaporated.

When cooked, fold in tomato pulp and cashews. Cook for another 10 minutes or until pulp is well blended in. Fill tomato shells with rice mixture and put into a baking dish.

Place lids on top of tomatoes. Bake in an oven preheated to 190°C (375°F) for 10 minutes. Serve tomatoes warm or chilled, garnished with parsley.

Serves 6

CHICKEN SALAD TACOS

6–8 taco shells
2 cups shredded lettuce or alfalfa
sprouts
200 g cold cooked chicken, cut
into strips
2 tomatoes, chopped
4 shallots, slivered
¾ cup grated Cheddar cheese
medium or hot taco sauce

Warm taco shells in the oven at 190°C (375°F) for 5 minutes or until crisp. Remove and cool. Fill each taco shell with lettuce, chicken, tomatoes and shallots. Top with grated cheese and sit wedged upright in an airtight container to transport. Serve taco sauce separately.

Serves 6–8

Springtime Salad

SWEET SURPRISES

For those who prefer salads a little on the sweet side, these recipes take full advantage of our juicy, succulent melons, pawpaws, grapes, peaches, pears and mangoes to devise brilliant salads for all seasons. From sweet and savoury dishes such as Green Pawpaw Salad to moulded iced puddings like Iced Summer Salad, these salads use skilful combinations to produce unusually delicious endings to any meal.

KIWI AND CASHEW SALAD

4 kiwi fruit, peeled and diced
2 oranges, peeled and segmented
few lettuce leaves
6 radishes, thinly sliced
100 g mushrooms, thinly sliced
small cucumber, thinly sliced
2 stalks celery, thinly sliced
¼ cup cashews
vinaigrette dressing (see recipe)

Toss all prepared ingredients in a salad bowl with nuts and vinaigrette dressing.

Serves 4

MELON, TOMATO AND CUCUMBER SALAD

500 g tomatoes
1 honeydew melon, diced
1 cucumber, diced
50 g lemon balm leaves

Cut tomatoes in halves then finely slice into half-moon shapes. Combine ingredients in salad bowl. Finely chop lemon balm leaves and sprinkle over salad. Chill well.

Serves 4–6

FESTIVE MELON SALAD

1 honeydew melon
1 rock melon
½ pawpaw
juice 2 limes
2 tablespoons finely chopped fresh coriander
5 tablespoons mayonnaise (see recipe)
3 tablespoons cream
24 thin slices proscuitto ham, halved

Halve and seed pips in fruits then, using an apple corer or melon baller, turn the 3 fruits into balls and place in a large glass bowl. Sprinkle liberally with lime juice and coriander. Cover and chill.

To serve, blend mayonnaise with cream and pour over fruit, taking care not to break melon balls. Fold proscuitto through last of all.

Note: Watermelon can be used for decorative purposes but is not recommended for use until the last moment as it tends to disintegrate if left too long in dressing.

Serves 12

GOLDEN GODDESS SALAD

2 large carrots, grated
1 crisp apple, peeled, cored and grated
juice 1 lime
2 tablespoons dried bananas
juice 1 orange
1 tablespoon clear honey
2 tablespoons preserved ginger, drained (not crystallised)
2 tablespoons pecan nuts

Combine all ingredients in a serving bowl, tossing well so that lime juice coats apple, and orange juice and honey cover other ingredients. Serve with cold chicken or turkey, diced and blended with a little curried mayonnaise. Allow 1 teaspoon curry with 2 tablespoons mayonnaise (see recipe), moistened with a little fresh cream, per 2 cups cold meat.

Serves 6

GREEN PAWPAW SALAD

5 tablespoons dried prawns
1 unripe pawpaw, peeled and
seeded
5 cloves garlic, peeled
1–2 red chillies, seeded
juice 2 limes
4–5 teaspoons anchovy sauce
4 firm lettuce leaves

Bring water to the boil and soak dried prawns for at least 30 minutes. Puree all ingredients together, adding more lime juice and/or anchovy sauce to taste if required. Serve in lettuce cups.

Serves 4

TROPICAL FISH AND FRUIT SALAD

500 g bream or snapper fish
¼ cup lemon juice
3 slices fresh pineapple, diced
6 guavas, stoned and diced
3 bananas, sliced
1 large firm ripe mango, peeled,
stoned and diced
1 onion, thinly sliced
1 red chilli, seeded and finely
chopped
¾ cup thick unsweetened
coconut milk
salt and freshly ground black
pepper
½ red capsicum, seeded and
finely sliced or snipped chives to
garnish

Cut fish into narrow strips and combine with lemon juice in a glass dish. Cover and refrigerate for at least 6 hours.

Drain and arrange fish and prepared fruit on a salad platter. Garnish with onion and chilli and pour over coconut milk. Season to taste and chill thoroughly. Garnish with red capsicum or chives. Coconut milk may be served separately if preferred.

Serves 4

FRUITED BURGHUL SALAD

2 cups water
1 cup burghul (cracked wheat)
1 cucumber, peeled and diced
1 cup chopped shallots, including
green part
½ cup chopped fresh mint
½ cup chopped fresh parsley
1 teaspoon salt
1 tablespoon chopped fresh
coriander
½ cup olive oil
½ cup lemon juice
4 fresh peaches or 8 dried
apricots (first swelled in hot
water and allowed to cool)
butter or mignonette lettuce
leaves

Pour boiling water over burghul and allow to stand for 45 minutes to swell. Strain and press out any excess liquid with the back of a spoon.

In a separate bowl place the next 6 ingredients. In a small bowl whisk olive oil with lemon juice, then combine with burghul and cucumber mixture. Refrigerate for at least two hours before serving.

Line a serving bowl with lettuce leaves. Dice the peaches or the apricots, blend into burghul mixture and fill lettuce lined dish to serve.

Serves 6

FLORIDA SALAD

2 apples, diced
3 tomatoes, diced
1 grapefruit, peeled and
segmented
2 oranges, peeled and segmented
2–3 tablespoons mayonnaise (see
recipe)
1 tablespoon sugar
1 tablespoon cream cheese
1 tablespoon chopped walnuts
lettuce leaves

Combine apples, tomatoes, grapefruit and oranges. Mix with remaining ingredients and chill thoroughly. Serve on bed of lettuce. Mayonnaise may be served separately.

Serves 4–6

SPICED PEARS IN BLANKETS

6 firm pears, peeled but kept
whole
1 carton lemon-flavoured
Philadelphia soft cheese or use
plain with lemon juice to taste
2 tablespoons cream
1 tablespoon paprika pepper
1 tablespoon finely chopped
chives
1 endive or another decorative
lettuce
2 tablespoons olive oil
juice ½ lime or ¼ lemon

Place pears in a pan with enough water to cover. Bring to the boil, lower heat and with lid firmly closed, simmer until tender but firm. Some pears soften quicker than others so test with a toothpick for tenderness. Remove to a platter and allow to cool.

Mix cheese with cream, paprika and chives. Using a spatula dipped in hot water, cover pears liberally with cheese mixture. Set on a bed of shredded lettuce first mixed lightly with oil and then sprinkled with lime juice.

Serves 6

PEAR SALAD

1 cup green grapes, halved and
seeded
1 cup chopped pineapple
1 cup chopped walnuts
4 large pears, peeled, halved
lengthways and cored
8 firm lettuce leaves

Sour Cream Dressing
1 cup sour cream
2 teaspoons sugar
1 tablespoon lemon juice
½ teaspoon dry mustard
¼ teaspoon paprika
pinch salt

Mix grapes, pineapple and walnuts together and press into pears. Serve in lettuce leaf cups with dressing. To make dressing, blend all ingredients together until well mixed.

Serves 8

Fruited Burghul Salad

SUMMER MANGO SALAD

¼ kg snow peas, topped and tailed
3 tablespoons mayonnaise (see recipe)
1 tablespoon cream
1 × 5 cm piece ginger root, finely chopped
1 tablespoon finely chopped mint leaves
2 × 260 g cans sliced water chestnuts, drained
2 ripe mangos, peeled and sliced

Place snow peas in steamer and cook for 3 minutes. Immediately plunge into iced water, drain, cover and store in refrigerator until required for assembly.

Blend the next 4 ingredients, cover and store in refrigerator. One hour before serving add water chestnuts to mayonnaise mixture. To serve, combine all ingredients in a glass bowl for best effect. This salad goes well with cold poultry accompanied by pecan and avocado salad (see recipe).

Summer Mango Salad

Serves 12

PRAWN AND PEAR SALAD

½ cup sour cream
75 g blue cheese eg blue vein
2 tablespoons lemon juice
1 clove garlic, crushed
½ teaspoon paprika
small mignonette lettuce, rinsed well
2 ripe pears, peeled, cored and quartered
200 g prawns, peeled, deveined and chilled

Combine the sour cream, blue cheese, lemon juice, garlic and paprika together in a bowl and beat until smooth. Remove the core from the lettuce and separate the leaves. Arrange leaves in a salad bowl and top with pears and prawns. Spoon over the dressing and serve.

Note: It is easy to mar the shape of the pear when removing cores — try halving the peeled pear and using a melon baller to scoop out the core.

Serves 4

Arzberg plate

PEARS IN TARRAGON DRESSING

3 ripe pears

Dressing
1 egg
2 tablespoons sugar
3 tablespoons tarragon vinegar
salt and freshly ground pepper
150 mL unflavoured yoghurt
6–12 lettuce leaves
½ teaspoon paprika

Beat egg in a small heat-proof bowl with a fork. Mix in sugar, then gradually add vinegar. Stand bowl over a pan of boiling water and whisk until mixture starts to thicken. Remove pan from heat and continue to whisk until mixture is the consistency of thickened cream. Remove bowl from water, whisk for a few seconds longer, season lightly and leave to cool completely. When it is cold, stir in the yoghurt.

Just before serving, peel, halve and core the pears. Arrange lettuce leaves on 6 individual serving dishes and place pears, cut side downwards, on top. Spoon sauce over, coating pears completely and sprinkle with a little paprika and pepper.

Serves 6

CLEOPATRA SALAD

250 g green grapes
250 g black grapes
12 strawberries
juice ½ lemon
2 tablespoons finely chopped fresh mint
5 tablespoons mayonnaise (see recipe)
2 tablespoons cream

Wash grapes and place in a salad bowl. Hull stawberries, halve, sprinkle with lemon juice and set aside. Blend mint with mayonnaise and cream. Pour over grapes and mix well. When ready to serve, top with strawberries. This salad travels well to picnics and is excellent with poultry or meats.

Serves 6

Top: Pears in Tarragon Dressing
Bottom: Cleopatra Salad

Arzberg plates

WATERMELON AND TURKEY SALAD

250 g roast turkey breast
½ cup pine nuts
1 butter or mignonette lettuce, washed and separated
¼ large watermelon, seeded and cut into chunks
5 shallots, thinly sliced
½ cup fresh coriander sprigs
6 tablespoons vinaigrette (see recipe)
freshly ground black pepper
½ cup mayonnaise (see recipe)

Cut turkey into strips. Toast pine nuts under the grill or in a dry frying pan until golden. Allow to cool. Arrange lettuce in the base of a large salad bowl and top with turkey, watermelon, shallots, pine nuts and coriander sprigs. Pour over vinaigrette and season with black pepper. Serve mayonnaise separately.

Serves 4

FIG AND PROSCUITTO SALAD

1 head of radicchio, washed and separated
8 fresh figs, quartered
200 g very thinly sliced proscuitto ham
6 tablespoons vinaigrette (see recipe) made with lemon juice and flavoured with garlic
freshly ground black pepper
few sprigs fresh tarragon

Line a large bowl with the radicchio leaves. Arrange the fig pieces over the lettuce and then the proscuitto ham. Pour the vinaigrette over the salad just before serving and season with freshly ground black pepper. Garnish with tarragon sprigs.

Serves 4

BLUEBERRY AND PINEAPPLE SALAD

1 ripe fresh pineapple, peeled and cored
1 punnet (250 g) blueberries
½ bunch shallots, slivered
½ cup fresh mint leaves
½ cup walnut pieces
6 tablespoons walnut oil
3 tablespoons pineapple juice
½ teaspoon Dijon-style mustard
salt and pepper
pinch brown sugar

Cut pineapple into chunks, reserving juice for dressing. Place pineapple chunks in a bowl with blueberries, shallots, mint and walnuts. Chill until ready to serve. Whisk walnut oil, pineapple juice and mustard together in a small bowl. Season with salt, pepper and sugar. Pour over salad 15 minutes before serving.

Serves 6

SUN SALAD

1 butter lettuce
1 ripe fresh pineapple, peeled, cored and thinly sliced
3 oranges, peeled and cut into segments
2 tomatoes, quartered
½ bunch shallots, sliced
½ cup sunflower seeds
½ cup sunflower seed sprouts (if available)
¼ cup red currants (if available)
4 tablespoons grapeseed oil
freshly ground black pepper
1 teaspoon raw sugar

Arrange lettuce over the base of a large bowl. Top with pineapple, orange segments, tomato and shallots. Scatter over sunflower seeds, sprouts and red currants. Whisk grapeseed oil together with black pepper and sugar. Pour over salad 15 minutes before serving.

Serves 6

ICED SUMMER SALAD

1 peach, diced
1 banana, diced
75 g strawberries, diced
2 teaspoons sugar
225 g cream cheese
½ teaspoon ground ginger
2 tablespoons lemon juice
2 tablespoons cream, whipped
¼ cup chopped hazelnuts
shredded lettuce
vinaigrette dressing (see recipe)

Sprinkle fruit with sugar. Blend cream cheese with ginger, lemon juice, then fold in cream, fruit and nuts. Pour mixture into 4 individual moulds and freeze for 1–2 hours, until firm. Dip each mould into hot water and turn salad out onto a bed of shredded lettuce. Serve immediately with vinaigrette dressing.

Serves 4

PECAN AND APPLE SALAD

2 red apples, halved, cored and cut into chunks
1 Granny Smith apple, halved, cored and cut into chunks
3 kiwi fruit, peeled and quartered
200 g Gruyere or Cheddar cheese, cut into matchsticks
¾ cup pecans
½ cup sultanas
⅓ cup Creme Fraiche or buttermilk
1 tablespoon lemon juice
salt and pepper
¼ teaspoon sugar
½ bunch chives, snipped

Place apples, kiwi fruit, cheese, pecans and sultanas in a serving bowl. Whisk Creme Fraiche or buttermilk with lemon juice and season with salt, pepper and sugar. Pour over salad and toss well. Garnish with chives.

Serves 4

Iced Summer Salad

FOR YOUR INFORMATION

Glossary of Terms

AUSTRALIA	UK	USA
Equipment and terms		
can	tin	can
crushed	minced	pressed
frying pan	frying pan	skillet
grill	grill	broil
greaseproof paper	greaseproof paper	waxproof paper
paper towel	kitchen paper	white paper towel
plastic wrap	cling film	plastic wrap
punnet	punnet	basket for 250 g fruit
seeded	stoned	pitted
Ingredients		
bacon rasher	bacon rasher	bacon slice
beetroot	beetroot	beets
black olive	black olive	ripe olive
calamari	squid	calamari
capsicum	pepper	sweet pepper
cornflour	cornflour	cornstarch
cream	single cream	light or coffee cream
crystallised fruit	crystallised fruit	candied fruit
desiccated coconut	desiccated coconut	shredded coconut
eggplant	aubergine	eggplant
five spice	Chinese spice combination of cinnamon, cloves, fennel, star anise and Szechuan pepper	
flour	plain flour	all-purpose flour
green cabbage	white or roundhead cabbage	cabbage
pawpaw	papaya	papaya or papaw
prawn	prawn or shrimp	shrimp
rock melon	ogen melon	cantaloupe
shallot	spring onion	scallion
snow pea	mangetout, sugar pea	snow pea
sour cream	soured cream	dairy sour cream
stock cube	stock cube	bouillon cube
sultanas	sultanas	seedless white or golden raisins
tasty cheese	mature Cheddar	Cheddar
rich cream	double cream	heavy or whipping cream
tomato puree	tomato puree	tomato paste
tomato sauce	tomato sauce	tomato ketchup
unsalted butter	unsalted butter	sweet butter
wholemeal flour	wholemeal flour	wholewheat flour
yoghurt	natural yoghurt	unflavoured yoghurt
zucchini	courgette	zucchini

If you need to substitute

Fresh fruit: replace with canned or tinned fruit.
Fresh herbs: replace with a quarter of the recommended quantity of dried herbs.
Dill can be replaced with fresh parsley, for a different flavour, but there is no substitute for fresh basil. Try growing some in summer in a pot.
Lebanese cucumber: Also called English, Cypress or telegraph cucumbers. Replace with any smooth-skinned cucumber.
Mulberries: replace with blackcurrants.
Pecans: replace with walnuts.
Rock melons: replace with honeydew melons.
Snapper or bream: replace with any firm white flesh fish including haddock, cod or whiting.

Oven Temperatures

	Celsius	Fahrenheit
Very slow	120	250
Slow	140–150	275–300
Moderately slow	160	325
Moderate	180	350
Moderately hot	190	375
Hot	200	400
	220	425
	230	450
Very hot	250–260	475–500

Measurements

Standard Metric Measures

1 cup	=	250 mL
1 tablespoon	=	20 mL
1 teaspoon	=	5 mL

All spoon measurements are level

Cup Measures

1 × 250 mL cup =	Grams	Ounces
breadcrumbs, dry	125	4½
soft	60	2
butter	250	8¾
cheese, grated cheddar	125	4½
coconut, desiccated	95	3¼
flour, cornflour	130	4¾
plain or self-raising	125	4½
wholemeal	135	4¾
fruit, mixed dried	160	5¾
honey	360	12¾
sugar, caster	225	7¾
crystalline	250	8¾
icing	175	6¾
moist brown	170	6
nuts	125	4

INDEX